Standout Virtual Events

How to create an experience
that your audience will love

David Meerman Scott
WITH
Michelle Manafy

Copyright © 2020 David Meerman Scott & Michelle Manafy

All rights reserved.

This publication may not be reproduced, sorted in a retrieval system, or transmitted in whole or in part, in any form or by any means, electronic, mechanical, photocopying, recording, or otherwise without permission of the authors.

CONTENTS

Introduction: **Making Connections in a Socially Distant World** — v

Chapter 1: **What Is The Purpose of Running a Virtual Event?** — 1
    Building fans of your organization with virtual events — 2
    Can the dynamic of in-person be recreated through virtual events? — 3
    Building fans with "proximity" at your virtual events — 5
    Video of people builds fandom in your business — 7

Chapter 2: **In-person vs. Virtual Events** — 9
    Swim into the torpedo — 9
    Virtual events are more like television than theater — 12
    It is critical to reimagine the presentation itself — 15
    The best virtual events reimagine what is possible rather than recreate what is familiar — 19
        Perspectives 2020 — 21
        Collision — 23
    Virtual events should be shorter — 25
        Scaling Up Summits — 26

Chapter 3: **Building Audience Interaction** — 29
    Using interactive features in your event platform — 30
    Social media #hashtags — 31
    Drive interaction at your virtual event — 33

Chapter 4: **Six Key Benefits to Hosting Virtual Events** — 37
    Build fans of your business — 39
    Reach massive audiences — 40
    Save time for attendees and speakers — 41
    Save money — 42
    Create unique, online experiences — 44
    Get better event feedback — 46

Chapter 5: **Format, Features and Platform Considerations** — 49
- Technology to host a virtual event — 49
  - Webinar software for basic events — 49
  - Integrated platforms for larger events — 51
  - Registration and participation management — 52
- Key considerations as you evaluate platforms for your large virtual event — 53
  - Pre-recorded vs. live — 54
  - Should you offer a replay of the sessions? — 58

Chapter 6: **Speaker Preparation for Virtual Events** — 61
- How different is it to give a speech virtually versus face-to-face? — 63
- Five common problems with virtual event speakers — 64
  - Speakers who are skilled at in-person events may not be skilled virtual speakers — 65
  - Virtual speakers may not have the right technology at home — 67
  - Virtual speakers might not involve the audience in their presentation — 69
  - Virtual event speakers don't forge a true partnership with event planners — 71
  - Virtual backgrounds are bad for your event's brand — 72
- The importance of a production team — 73
- How speakers and producers work together to make an event great — 75
- Provide your speakers with guidelines and guidance — 77

Chapter 7: **The Business of Virtual Events** — 81
- Types of virtual events — 81
  - Basic webinars offered at no charge to participants — 81
  - Simple events where you charge a fee — 82
  - Larger events with multiple tracks — 82
- Pricing your Virtual Event — 83
  - Fully paid virtual event — 83
  - Do you want many more people exposed to your ideas? Make it free! — 84
  - A hybrid free and paid approach — 84
- Sponsors — 85
  - Simple webinar sponsorship — 85
  - Larger events with a single sponsor — 86

Larger events or event-series with multiple sponsors	86
Marketing and promotion	89
Create a great virtual event page or site	89
Generate links to the landing page in as many ways as you can	90
Social networking from you, your speakers, and partners	91
Consider an affiliate program for paid events	91
Art and science	91

Chapter 8: **The Cost of Producing a Virtual Event** — 93
- Webinar platform costs — 94
- Virtual event platform costs — 94
- Virtual event technology and studio costs — 96
- Virtual event speaker fees — 97

Chapter 9: **How to Run A Great Virtual Event** — 99
- Identify your goals and measure success — 99
  - Revenue generator — 99
  - Building fans of your organization — 100
  - Generating sales leads — 101
- Big picture planning — 102
  - Create a checklist — 102
  - Your event timeline — 103
- It's go time — 103

Acknowledgements — 105

About The Authors — 108

INTRODUCTION:

Making Connections in a Socially Distant World

In just the first two months of 2020, David delivered talks to thousands of people at 10 different in-person events on three continents.

Michelle's organization had a dozen events planned for the year, topics set, locations booked, contracts signed. And she'd already agreed to participate in many others.

Then Covid-19 hit. David's last in-person speaking engagement in 2020 was on March 3. Mid-March, Michelle's organization sent everyone home and went into wait-and-see mode. Both quickly realized that for the foreseeable future, there would be no in-person events.

David found himself in a bit of a daze when the in-person events industry vanished. For more than a decade, he had been used to delivering 30 or 40 presentations a year all over the world, racking up hundreds of thousands of air miles as he shared ideas about how organizations of all kinds create marketing strategies that turn customers into fans.

Michelle found herself part of a team that had produced live events together for many years, but with little experience in virtual events. Given the emotional, personal, and professional impact of Covid-19, some members were slow to abandon hope for the return of physical events. However, she could see that there was a need to quickly explore virtual options and build a plan.

Once he overcame his initial shock that the events business had dramatically changed, seemingly overnight, David became super excited and hopeful as he began testing many new ways to deliver content to people online. And within weeks, his work shifted to exclusively digital. Between April 2 and the end of September, when this book was completed, he delivered talks at 25 virtual events. Within a few short weeks, Michelle created a plan to shift her organization's events online, including rethinking their structure, timeline, sponsorships and more, which she pitched to key stakeholders, who jumped in to make the shift.

Both David and Michelle were quick to see that the events business — and their careers — were transforming in real time. In our own ways, and then together, we dug into the art and science of virtual events and looked at how to produce effective virtual events from every angle. And these explorations became the ideas you will read here.

As speakers at and organizers of virtual events, we had unique opportunities to learn from many different aspects of the events business. We spoke with virtual event organizers, event production companies, speaker bureaus, virtual event platform companies and broadcast studios, as well as attendees, sponsors, and speakers at virtual events.

We studied what makes virtual events great as well as common problems and shortcomings. We focused on what makes for a wonderful virtual presentation. And we explored the technology required and the costs of hosting a virtual event.

Once we both realized that we had amassed a unique knowledge base very quickly, this short book was born to share what we have learned with event organizers, companies considering a virtual event, speakers, and others. The goal: To help everyone produce truly great virtual events.

This guide will take event planners through understanding the basics of virtual events, including how to choose the right platform, pick the best speakers, help all of your speakers better perform in a virtual setting, figure out what costs are involved, promote your event, and consider how to avoid common shortfalls of virtual events.

For virtual event speakers, we discuss how to deliver a great talk, how to be a good partner to event organizers and how to interact with your audience.

Whether you are a seasoned event organizer or speaker making the transition to virtual events, or just getting your first event off the ground, this guide will equip you with everything you need for success.

On a personal note, we are thrilled to be working together

again. Michelle was David's very first editor nearly 20 years ago, when he was a cub contributing editor at *EContent* magazine. Around that time, David spoke on a panel that Michelle moderated at the Buying and Selling EContent conference in Scottsdale, Arizona. Soon, they were collaborating on other projects including David's 2005 book *Cashing in with Content*, which Michelle edited.

We want to thank the many organizations that have stepped up to create high quality virtual events at a time when many of us are hungry to learn new things, and who were kind to share their experiences with us. This steep learning curve has been tough for organizers and speakers alike. But these skills will pay off in the short and long term.

We are both firmly convinced that virtual events are here to stay, even when in-person events can resume. While in-person events will certainly return, we think many events will move to a hybrid model with some people gathered in a physical venue and others coming together online. The advantages of virtual events are clear. They offer incredible flexibility along with emerging advantages and opportunities.

We have organized the content into chapters and within each chapter there are sections. You don't have to read this book cover to cover, or in order, for it to be useful. For some readers, it might be more helpful to dip in and out of the chapters and sections that most closely meet your needs and interests. Whether you read front to back, or start with your most pressing needs or interests, we believe you will find useful insights and advice that will help you be a driving force behind creating standout virtual events that attendees will love.

CHAPTER 1

What Is The Purpose of Running a Virtual Event?

From corporate gatherings, industry meetings and roadshows, to trade shows and massive expos, events have been around forever. They provide an opportunity to bring people together to share knowledge and learn from one another. Attendees can network and make new professional contacts while corporations can demonstrate their products and knowledge to potential customers. Along the way, connections are made, business is built, and if things go right, everyone leaves feeling like the event was worth the time, money and effort.

Of course, for many organizations, events are a business unto themselves. There are entire industries built around conferences, huge venues dedicated to hosting them, and a whole slew of interconnected industries that do production, light and sound, provide meals, book speakers, and other critical components.

Virtual events are not a new thing either. With the advent of digital, virtual events cropped up. The old-school webinar (web-based seminar), for example, has been around for well over a decade. However, with the shutdown of in-person events starting in early

2020, many organizations were pushed to rethink what would be possible if people could not travel or gather in large groups.

Given the size of the events industry and the revenue at stake, it is no surprise that some organizations have turned an eye to the potential of virtual events. The trouble is that when people think of virtual events, those old-school webinars are the first thing that springs to mind. While they are a good way to share knowledge and even generate revenue, webinars can hardly supplant the entire events industry in terms of revenue or experience.

That said, virtual events have tremendous potential to create fans of the organizations that host them. Done well, a virtual event can be the best marketing a company can do all year. Big issues can be addressed by convening global experts. More sales leads can be generated through these types of initiatives than through any others. Non-profits can secure donations. Trade associations and other organizations can maintain member satisfaction.

Building fans of your organization with virtual events

In 2015 David began to dig deep into the idea of fandom. He looked at how and why people become a fan of a company, a product, a service, or an idea. We learned that much of fandom is rooted in neuroscience, which explains the power of events to build fans and grow business. Events offer a unique opportunity to build and reinforce "Fanocracy," a concept coined by David explored in more depth in the Wall Street Journal bestselling book *Fanocracy: Turning Fans into Customers and Customers into Fans* (2020, Portfolio/Penguin Random House), co-authored with his daughter, Reiko.

David and Reiko spoke with neuroscientists to understand what goes on in our brains when we connect with other people. It turns out that we humans are hard-wired to want to be part of a tribe of like-minded people. That is where we feel safe and comfortable. This concept is an important survival technique because when we are with people who we know and trust, we are safe. When we are with people we do not know, we can feel vulnerable. This goes back thousands of years and explains why humans live in groups.

That is why when you are with your friends you feel great and when you are in a crowded elevator you might feel vulnerable. It is also why you enjoy interacting with people at an in-person event, because everyone is there to learn from one another. A tribe is built by the organization hosting the event and people want to return year after year.

But can that experience be replicated or experienced virtually? We think so. However, it is not simply a question of dusting off a conference program and porting it online.

Can the dynamic of in-person be recreated through virtual events?

To go even deeper into the neuroscience of developing fans, it is important to look at a simple but frequently overlooked dynamic in our digital age: virtual proximity.

It is not always possible to bring people together in-person, a fact that became a stark reality in 2020. However, an understanding of the power of proximity is important background to the concept of virtual proximity, which we can build with video as part of a virtual event.

To really understand virtual proximity, we need to look at the importance to all humans of in-person proximity to like-minded people.

What is it about being around other people that we humans crave? Why is physical proximity so important? Cultural anthropologist Edward T. Hall started studying this phenomenon in the 1950s.

Dr. Hall defined humans' use of physical space in a simple way in his 1966 book *The Hidden Dimension* where he describes how people like to keep certain distances between themselves and others. It explores how our use of space can affect our personal and business relations and explains why in-person events are so powerful.

To be effective communicators, we need to learn how to consciously manage the physical space between ourselves and others.

The significance of each level of proximity can be predicted and managed to create the most optimal outcomes. For instance, Hall described "public distance" as more than 12 feet away from others. When somebody is further than 12 feet from us, our unconscious brains know they are there, but we do not actively track them. He identified "social distance" for interactions among acquaintances, such as walking the exhibit hall at in-person events, as being from four feet to 12 feet. We unconsciously track people who enter our social space because our ancient brains want to know if there is danger among those people. "Personal distance" for interactions among good friends or business contacts ranges from about a foot and a half to four feet, which would occur at meal breaks or the reception at an event.

Understanding these degrees of human proximity at in-person events and how they predict shared emotional connections with others has an enormous effect on building fans at an event. People who are able to cultivate physical closeness by engaging with them face-to-face can create stronger emotional bonds. At the same time, attendees cannot help but feel uncomfortable when walking the exhibit floor if a booth representative approaches them, getting too close in an unwanted way, because it is hardwired in us to be wary.

Normally, when we are able to interact together, the most rewarding encounters in our lives occur within our social space and personal space. It is one of the reasons in-person events are so popular.

Building fans with "proximity" at your virtual events

People go to an in-person event for more than the programming — they go to enjoy close proximity with other like-minded people.

So far, we have looked at the importance of in-person human connection to grow fans. However, not all businesses can have that kind of connection with every would-be fan. And as we write this, in-person events have essentially stopped because of the pandemic.

So, given travel limitations or because your audience is spread out all over the world, how can your business achieve similar success?

It turns out that virtual events can still deliver the power of connection through another fascinating form of what neuroscience called "mirror neurons." Mirror neurons are a group of cells in the premotor cortex and inferior parietal cortex of our brain. That is a mouthful of scientific language!

To keep it simple, these neurons offer some valuable insights for virtual event speakers and planners. They not only activate when we perform an action — biting into a lemon, smiling — but they also fire when we observe somebody else performing the same action. For instance, when those around us are happy and smiling, our unconscious brain tells us that we are happy. Often, we will also smile.

A critical aspect of understanding mirror neurons is remembering that it is how we humans are hardwired. Our ancient brain is at work helping us cope with the world around us, protecting us from danger and keeping us healthy. We are not able to choose to turn on or choose to ignore.

We cannot help but react the way we do.

Here is where it gets really interesting for the virtual events business: People unconsciously bond with people they see on screens and on-stage as if we were together with them in-person because of mirror neurons. This helps to explain why we feel that we "know" movie stars and television personalities. We have seen those actors or commentators on a screen as if they were in our personal space, inside of four feet, and our brain gives us the feeling that we have actually met them.

The same thing is true for virtual events. If a speaker's video is cropped effectively and she looks directly at the camera and presents in a warm and familiar tone, audience members will develop a powerful bond with her. These positive virtual connections serve to make those people fans of your business.

Video of people builds fandom in your business

A deeper understanding of mirror neurons can help you build fans within your organization, or market any products and services you want to sell by hosting virtual events. Businesses can use the concept of mirror neurons to build fans in many ways. One important aspect is creating connections via our virtual toolset.

Video of people, as part of a virtual event, is a fabulous way to reach people emotionally though the power of mirror neurons. However, watching an actor perform is quite different than seeing one in a brilliant fireside chat, or breaking down the fourth wall and communicating directly with the audience.

As in face to face encounters, there is something truly profound about eye contact and focused attention. When you shoot video for a virtual event, ensure that speakers look directly into the camera and adopt a friendly and open approach.

Beyond employing talented speakers and producers to ensure that virtual connections are enabled, it will take creativity to build lasting connections among attendees. You will need to consider ways to connect fans with each other, with the speakers, and with your business. As with an in-person event, fostering social connections is critical for a virtual event's success.

CHAPTER 2

In-person vs. Virtual Events

Why do some virtual events succeed while others miss the mark?

One likely reason is that organizations simply try to recreate the in-person event they are familiar with digitally. Unfortunately, they fail to find the right medium and methodology for virtual success.

Swim into the torpedo

"The biggest thing we've learned is that when you are in a situation like this: You cannot simply translate by taking all the magical moments that happened in the in-person events and try to recreate things like an expo, and the hotel lobby bar. You really have to reinvent," said Bob Bejan, the corporate vice president: global events, production studios and marketing community at Microsoft. "You just have to let it all go. You have to say what I'm trying to do is make human connections. What I'm trying to do is make people more knowledgeable and understand more. And we're trying to make people understand that they are part of something bigger than themselves. The root of these online experiences is about that, not how to create a perfect expo booth or a perfect keynote."

In the second week of March 2020, Microsoft went from a strong focus on in-person event experiences, some for tens of thousands of people at a time, to cancelling 32 global events, taking almost all of them into the digital world. "That kind of transformation is pretty radical," said Bejan. "When you think about taking all the experiences that we know about and all of the things we've done for years and years and transforming them to a different medium, the learning curve has been very steep. What's incredible is that when groups of people get forced into these situations, if you are willing to let yourself have your mind opened, it can create an enormously creative cycle. And that's what's happened at Microsoft."

David co-presented at Microsoft Inspire with Bejan on July 22 in a session titled *Digital experiences in a pandemic era – connecting with customers when it is hard to connect*. Their talk focused on how to make a quick shift to digital communications.

"During times of adversity, how do you unlock the creativity that's required to respond effectively? I think the answer is to cultivate a discipline of design thinking and develop a culture where you embrace failure," Bejan said about the strategies he uses at Microsoft. "What we say in our team is 'swim into the torpedo'. Our entire team thinks it's better to accelerate into the problem. We cultivate that and it takes discipline because you can blow yourself up. It's like athletics, you have to do it every day. If you do that you can respond to difficult problems like the pandemic."

While some powerful elements are lost when an event moves from a hotel ballroom or conference center to a computer screen or smartphone, there are other aspects that are optimized and superior online.

"The digital medium is way better than in-person for certain things like delivering information verbally together with additional supporting material and driving you to action," Bejan said. "This is more effective in the digital world. All of us in the events business have been lazy for the past decade about not thinking about the power of digital in combination with in-person. That's been quite a revelation and humbling, I think. It's so easy to get lazy."

The switch to an entirely digital event schedule from March 2020 has been demanding for Bejan and his team at Microsoft. However, by rethinking the entire events program and "swimming into the torpedo," the efforts have proven to be extremely valuable for Microsoft customers, partners, and employees.

"The power of the human spirit to connect with another one has been the biggest challenge as we explore and move ourselves forward as we learn how to communicate in a digital world. How do you make these emotional connections? Our feedback from the audiences at our digital events has been crazily, overwhelmingly positive" said Bejan.

As you make the transition to virtual events like Microsoft has done, start with your audience. Think about what they need and what value you plan to deliver. Consider their desires and expectations. Then, consider budget and objectives.

It is possible to find the optimal intersection and deliver a virtual event that will delight audiences, build fans, and add to the bottom line. But the worst mistake you can make it to begin from a place of "we have always done it this way." While you can deliver much of the value of an in-person event in virtual, the tools and tactics are different.

Virtual events are more like television than theater

In a theatrical performance, the audience is present. Their feedback is immediate and palpable. You know right away whether your performance is resonating. You are on the big stage and have to play big and bold to connect with those in the back row. Lighting, sound and production value all come into play and they can enhance or detract from a presentation.

Stage performers sometimes struggle to transition to the screen because of the proximity to the camera and the lack of an in-person audience. Production values matter, but they are far from the same as those in a theater. Playing to a camera is very different from reacting to — and interacting with — a physical crowd. Yet without a doubt, connections can be made, and audiences can be informed and entertained. It is, however, a question of mastering a new medium.

It probably will not come as a big surprise that — given our work in and around the media industry — we have a fascination with the inner workings of the business. Longtime readers will recall David's book, *Marketing the Moon*, which inspired a three-part PBS American Experience mini-series called *Chasing the Moon* (for which he served as a consulting producer). David had the incredible experience of introducing the filmmaker Robert Stone to Apollo 11 astronaut Buzz Aldrin and then interviewing Aldrin for the project.

David has also dabbled in a bit of, well, shall we say "acting." If you blinked, you probably missed him in feature films like *American Hustle*, reality shows like *Space Dealers*, and television commercials for companies like Toshiba.

Michelle works with dozens of media companies and is privileged to hear their stories from the front lines of production including the challenges of working across a wide range of mediums. It is incredibly fun to see how the magic is made — even from the sidelines.

A network television morning program, for example, has producers who work hard on developing substantive content well before filming takes place. This type of production includes a host, who sets the scene and keeps things on track, and features guests who appear live or on pre-recorded segments. They are sometimes on site or appear remotely. (Having been interviewed as an expert on news shows from networks like CNN, MSNBC, and FOX many times, David has seen this from behind the scenes.)

Virtual event producers should take note of the processes involved in this type of production. Many organizations provide media training for their executives; being "camera ready" means a

"This is funny!", a self-conscious virtual speaker might say into the silence, "You're supposed to laugh at this!"

To deliver a powerful virtual presentation, speakers need to think about their art in a different way.

At the same time, event producers need to reimagine what is possible and choose speakers accordingly.

"It's obvious that choosing a speaker for a virtual event is different from choosing one for an in-person event," said Tony D'Amelio. A 50-year veteran in representing talent for live events, Tony is principal of D'Amelio Network, a boutique speaker management firm that represents David as well as Bob Woodward, Ron Insana, Bill Walton, Katty Kay, and others.

"When we were all thrust into the virtual events world in early 2020, I heard too many people focusing on the negative — that virtual was flat and couldn't create the excitement of an in-person experience," D'Amelio said. "To me, those comments were excuses to not confront reality. The truth is, virtual events are just different. They have unique qualities. And whether they connect with and engage the audience comes down to careful preparation by a speaker."

Knowing when to pause on stage at a critical point during a talk and deliver a well-rehearsed line by walking forward a few steps, giving the audience a beat to react: all part of the performance. Reading an audience, feeding on their reactions and expectations, this all yields a powerful experience. But none of this is possible in a virtual talk.

"I received some advice in early 2020 that helped me put virtual speaking events in context," D'Amelio said. "Every attendee at a virtual event has a front row seat, someone said to me. The speaker doesn't need to project to the back row – that theatrical model is for in-person events. The virtual model is cinematic; a whisper can be as powerful as a shouting voice. So right there, what you're looking for in a speaker is very different from an in-person event."

If you are a speaker making the transition to speaking at virtual events, you will need to re-work your entire talk. The first step is to break the existing talk into chunks of about five to seven minutes. In this way, a 45-minute in-person keynote will become a virtual talk of six or eight sections. To mix up the format of the sections, speakers can use the breakout room feature if the platform has one, conduct a poll and analyze the results, show a short video and describe learnings from it, and conduct a short live interview, all in one talk. If a speaker can do all of those things in 45 minutes, the talk will be quite different from an in in-person talk, but it is dynamic and engaging in a way that is ideal for a screen.

Given the differences between in-person speaking techniques and what works in a virtual event, how do event planners choose virtual speakers?

"The first issue is assessing how comfortable they are speaking to a camera," D'Amelio said. "It's not for everyone. Just like you would for in-person, get video samples of virtual events the speaker has spoken to."

What can be done if an event must feature a company executive or sponsor without good virtual speaking skills or if the planning team is set on a speaker who does not have the chops? If event planners have a speaker that they want to use but who is not comfortable on camera, an interview with a skilled moderator like Michelle who can guide the conversation can be a terrific solution. Journalists make terrific interviewers and many have experience in front of a camera. Academics and subject matter experts may also be well suited to drawing out the interviewee. It will be critical to ensure that a panel moderator or interviewer for a fireside chat is highly comfortable with the subject matter, the medium, and confident enough to lead the discussion if it lulls or heads off track.

"A speaker who is not comfortable on camera shouldn't automatically disqualify them. The secret weapon for virtual events is conversation," D'Amelio said. "I'm convinced an experienced moderator or interviewer can make a camera-shy speaker feel comfortable and also make sure that the most relevant information is excavated. Certainly, two people in conversation is more engaging than just one talking head."

The best virtual events reimagine what is possible rather than recreate what is familiar

To be clear: A virtual event is neither a digital replica of an in-person event, nor is it network news or a daytime talk show. Elements of each will impact the design of an event. But to build your best virtual event, you need to rethink what is possible.

It is human nature for us to take what we already know from an offline world and apply it online. Over the decades we have both spent working in digital businesses we have seen countless initiatives fail as they try to recreate online what they are used to in the offline world.

Advertising agencies missed the web marketing revolution by focusing on annoying and interruptive ads. However, smart advertisers recognized that digital affords them unprecedented consumer understanding and the ability to deliver desirable information at the right time, in the right context.

Newspaper companies nearly missed the online information revolution because they focused on recreating their print newspaper online. Magazines almost made the same mistake, but successful ones realized that consumers behave differently online and that there are experiences that lend themselves better to digital. And digitally native media organizations sprang up that intuitively understood the medium.

Our challenge with online events and virtual speaking is to focus on what is possible, not on trying to replicate what we already know.

The best virtual events are more than televised keynotes. They must go beyond the charismatic talking head. The best virtual events create a compelling and engaging digital experience. The key is that we need to use the power of the online medium rather than trying to recreate an offline experience. David created a six minute video that he published to Vimeo that goes into detail on these ideas: *Virtual Events vs In-Person Events: How Do They Compare?*

For example, great events include ways for the audience to interact with one another. Networking is one of the main reasons people attend in-person events. Unfortunately, at your average webinar, there is not a lot of introducing yourselves to those seated nearby, or hallway serendipity.

However, successful virtual events will leverage digital tools to enable networking, maybe even more effectively than in-person networking. Through different tools built into virtual event platforms attendees can chat with one another, live, as a speaker is presenting. We will discuss this in more detail in Chapter 3.

Presenters can use a breakout room feature as part of their talk, to put attendees into small groups of five or six people so they can interact for a few minutes about the subject being discussed.

And after a talk, virtual meeting rooms can be set up where people who share common challenges and goals can collaborate based on the information they just learned. Events can offer "speed dating" tools that allow for attendees to randomly interact with peers for short spans. That idea can be further refined by matchmaking around specified interests. This can even serve as a premium upsell if attendees are given the opportunity to interact with speakers, or sponsors are given the chance to meet with potential customers, for example.

Perspectives 2020

Like many in-person client conferences, Skillsoft moved its *Perspectives 2020* event online. Rather than just taking its existing content and putting it on the web, Skillsoft, a global leader in learning and talent management solutions, completely rethought what was possible.

"Reimagining Perspectives during a pandemic couldn't be as simple as doing a broadcast version of our in-person event; it needed to reflect our new brand and frankly our vision to democratize learning," Michelle Boockoff-Bajdek, Skillsoft's chief marketing officer told us, "which meant that we had to create something new that encouraged people — everyone — to participate live. And so, our marketing team and agency partners spent 28 hours over two days in a design-thinking workshop determining what would make for a best-in-class live digital experience, drawing inspiration from some of the most unexpected places."

Normally, the Skillsoft Perspectives in-person customer conference held each May draws 1,000 participants.

In 2020 Skillsoft made a bold move for their virtual event. They chose a 24-hour "follow the sun" approach to entice a global audience. Perspectives 2020 kicked off on May 13 at 9:00 am Sydney time and included speakers such as author of Educated Tara Westover, panels, case studies and other programming that originated in Sydney, Singapore, Delhi and London, and concluded at 6:30 p.m. Boston time with David's keynote. David made a five-minute highlight video of the virtual event: *Virtual Keynote Speaker David Meerman Scott Highlights from Skillsoft Perspectives 2020 from David Meerman Scott* on Vimeo.

The event was highly engaging, for the full 24 hours. "We packed it with everything leaders and learners need to upskill and reskill for whatever their future holds," said Boockoff-Bajdek. "The level of engagement and the studio chat was off the charts. And it's because of the content — a stellar roster of keynotes, moderated panels between practitioners and experts on the topic of Business Continuity Planning, hosted (and heated!) head-to-head debates in each region; and moments of infotainment that kept people tuning in."

Throughout the day, David served as co-host with Boockoff-Bajdek. She was the leader of the event while David jumped in with "color commentary" from time to time. Using hosts brought consistency to Skillsoft Perspectives 2020 and kept audiences tuned in for what was coming next.

Skillsoft Perspectives 2020 also included a live musical performance by Kev Sylvester and Wil Baptiste of Black Violin, who played from their studio in Florida. David interviewed Wil and Kev after their performance from the Boston studio and the interplay between the artists, who were both in their studio, was popular with attendees.

The results of Skillsoft's first virtual customer conference were impressive. "We set high stretch targets for the digital event hoping to drive 20 times the registration that we would have seen for an in-person event," Boockoff-Bajdek says. "We more than doubled those numbers, hitting 42,000 total registrants with a 37 percent attendance rate. We drove real-time engagement from participants: more than 1.4 million minutes of content were consumed over the course of 24-hours. And tens of thousands of people took advantage of our trial offer, gaining unrestricted access to all of the content available in Skillsoft's *Percipio*, our learning experience platform."

Collision

Michelle (Manafy) was slated to be a host of the Content Maker's stage at Collision, North America's fastest-growing tech conference, which was originally planned as an in-person event in Toronto, Canada. In just 12 weeks, their team turned a physical conference virtual.

When the producers realized they needed to shift to virtual, they leaned heavily into a "TV-like" model. This involved recording hundreds of talks in advance of the air date, which allowed them to optimize recording quality, lighting, sound, etc. They offered one free channel and two premium ones as well as an audio-only "radio" channel and highlights from past events. In the end they produced more than 150 hours of original content.

Collision absolutely did not want to forgo the excitement and engagement of their past events. They employed a number of interactive digital elements, as well as airing live segments alongside the pre-recorded ones. Talks included the ability to rate speakers in real time as well as a chat function that let attendees interact with one another. Several of the most well-known speakers who had produced their talks ahead of time also participated in live interactive Q&A sessions.

Collision also held an Irish Pub night for press in attendance. Whereas previous years saw press shuttled on busses to various private events all over the host city, this year they brought press together for a drink in their home country, Ireland, virtually. Press who registered to attend were shipped a box of Tullamore D.E.W. Irish Whiskey, Angostura bitters, simple syrup, and lemons. Attendees joined a Zoom call live from Tullamore's distillery where they were guided through the distillery's history and how to make three cocktail recipes, and entertained by a popular pub performer.

The event allowed press to interact with one another, enjoy a couple of cocktails and a live performance, and created a highly favorable impression for both Tullamore and Collision. And let's face it: That last bit is one of the primary reasons press are invited to conferences in the first place.

Virtual events should be shorter

Typical in-person events range in length from a full day to a week or more, with programming starting in the morning each day and frequently running through an after-party late into the night. Keynotes and panel discussions are usually an hour in length and "blocks" of programming time are usually 90 minutes to two or three hours, with networking and meal breaks in between.

That model works when people are physically together in a convention center or hotel ballroom, but it is not ideal for virtual events. Shorter usually works better with virtual because people tend to multitask when participating in a virtual event and many people are familiar with consuming short form content online, such as YouTube videos.

Ideally, virtual event programming will include some shorter 15 to 20-minute session. If you have longer keynotes, you can break them up into modules with the Q&A coming after a short break. Consider a typical network news program and how it is broken into segments with commercial breaks coming at regular intervals. While you do not need commercials in your virtual event, you do need to break up content into shorter segments.

At a recent event where David spoke, there were five-minute breaks built in every 45 minutes or so. During some breaks, a yoga instructor led interested people in some stretching exercises. Programmers also included a live webcam of some goats with a farmer talking about them, courtesy of a company called Goat to Meeting.

Scaling Up Summits

As you reimagine what is possible with your virtual event, do not be afraid to make some radical changes. David spoke at a Scaling Up Summit organized by Verne Harnish, author and founder/CEO of a global executive education and coaching firm Scaling Up and hosted by *Chief Executive Magazine*. Their virtual event was all about short form — really short form.

"When the pandemic hit in March, within two weeks we pivoted from our in-person two-day Summits to asking top thought leaders and CEOs to deliver in just 10 minutes what they might take an hour to share at an in-person event," said Harnish. "We shared the equivalent amount of insights, ideas, and inspiration in two-hours, compared to what would normally consume two-days of attendees time, not including the time and expense of travel. As such, 94 percent of our audience asked for more structured events like this given the time constraints we're all experiencing in the face of the pandemic."

As with other virtual events we have discussed in these pages, the key for Harnish was not trying to replicate his company's two-day format online. Instead he compacted it into just two hours.

Harnish's team followed up each of the events with professionally created notes as well as links to watch replays of individual presentations as an added value for attendees. They offered the replays as a paid option for those who could not attend live, generating more revenue for the event.

As a speaker at several of Harnish's new, very short virtual events, David can say with certainty that the 10-minute speaker format was a hit with attendees. After his brief talk, David's social media feeds lit up with people who had attended the summit thanking him for his session and wanting to engage further with the ideas he presented.

It was a success for Harnish and his team too because they sold thousands of tickets at an average of $95 each. In fact, the 12 speaker, 10-minutes-each format was so popular that Scaling Up have replicated the it three more times with celebrity speakers including Richard Branson, Mark Cuban, Nate Blecharczyk, Margaret Heffernan, Sarah Friar, General Stanley McChrystal, Greg Brenneman and more. They've also featured top business books authors including bestsellers Gary Hamel, Susan David, Adam Grant, Scott Galloway, Hermann Simon and Keith Ferrazzi.

"These events allowed us to reach new people who joined as a participant as well as broaden our reach of sponsors, partners, and affiliate arrangements," said Harnish. "Whereas we expected around 1,000 CEOs and CXOs to attend our in-person event, we hosted over 14,000 paid attendees across the four virtual summits. So, our reach was essentially 12 times our in-person events and we were able to replace most of our gross margin dollars."

The Scaling Up team are planning additional virtual events using the same formula in late 2020 and into 2021.

Harnish added: "As Margaret Heffernan suggested in her

opening remarks of the first virtual event we hosted 'now is the time to be ambitious!'"

Remember, many audience members will have the expectation of past live events when they sign up for your virtual event. While you certainly don't want to try to replicate in-person online, you want to satisfy one of the biggest reasons people attend events: the ability to build a tribe through shared interests and interaction, something we will cover in the next chapter.

CHAPTER 3

Building Audience Interaction

While a great virtual event is more like television than theater, that is not the whole story. If you only focus on the TV part, you miss the opportunity for the audience interaction. The reality is that online consumer expectations have been highly shaped by social media. Thus, they expect real-time interaction, along with time-shifted or on-demand experiences.

One of the best aspects of an in-person event is an audience being together, interacting, learning from one another and making professional connections. When people meet at the meals, coffee breaks, receptions, or while waiting for a keynote to start, a powerful tribe of like-minded people can develop.

People come back to an in-person event year after year because an organization has built a "Fanocracy" around their event. The challenge for online events is to develop that tribe. To do so, they must facilitate interaction among like-minded people.

The same thing is true about virtual events. People come together around an interesting topic and interact with speakers and one another. And that is an important key to successful virtual events: real-time audience interaction.

If one-way broadcast events were enough, we could all just tune into TED talks, which are interesting and valuable (and free). The TED YouTube channel has nearly 18 million subscribers. But a TED talk is different than a live virtual event because it lacks audience interaction.

Most virtual events fail to provide audience interaction because they simply try to recreate the stage experience from a physical event. They deliver a passive experience for the audience. So, they miss ways to use online tools to develop interaction between people.

Using interactive features in your event platform

If you do focus on offering live virtual sessions, there are a number of ways to involve the audience in a virtual presentation. However, keep in mind that each virtual event platform is different. Some offer a full suite of interactive features while others do not. Zoom, for example offers the possibility of putting a subset of attendees into breakout rooms for more intimate discussions. This can be much like what would occur at a round table of six or eight people over lunch at an in-person event. Other platforms, however, do not offer this feature.

Michelle has used breakout rooms to provide focus groups around specific areas of interest or concern. For example, with a panel discussion, each panelist might lead specific breakouts with small groups of attendees as a premium value add.

Chat is another feature offered by most virtual event platforms. David likes to immediately start out his talks by asking people to share something that they are a fan of. It could be a band, a sports team, something they like to do for exercise, a company, a product. Attendees type this into the chat feature of whichever events platform is being used. As people's fandoms scroll by, he reads some out loud, and of course, the audience can read along as well and see others' responses. This gets the audience involved from the first minutes of the talk.

If an event platform includes a polling feature, David might pop up a poll every 10 minutes or so. Michelle finds polls particularly useful before a session goes to Q&A to get people buzzing about something thought provoking or controversial from a talk.

Capitalizing on the features of the virtual event platform changes what would otherwise be a one-way delivery of content to be an interactive experience involving each audience member.

Social media #hashtags

Social media is another great way to get people involved. For example, Twitter is an ideal back channel for people to communicate before, during and after a virtual event.

The key is choosing a unique hashtag that will aggregate all the tweets of people who use that hashtag into one feed so people can see what is happening in real-time. Many virtual event planners with good intentions choose a hashtag that is already being used by another event or for another purpose. Make sure you do a search on Twitter and other social networks for that hashtag to see if it is already being used. You want to your hashtag to be unique to your event or event series.

Some events use the same hashtag for their in-person events year after year while others create a unique hashtag each year, typically by adding the year after the event name. Sometimes, a hashtag grows organically as people gravitate towards it so keep in mind that there may be more than one active hashtag around your event. For example, as we write this, HubSpot's virtual INBOUND 2020 event is about to get underway. People who are eager to attend are using both #Inbound and #Inbound2020 hashtags. We have even seen a few people using #Inbound20.

Ideally, you would choose a hashtag as early as possible, preferably before you announce your event. Then, mention the hashtag in all your communications as you launch your virtual event, on the event website, and in all your social media posts, and emails to attendees. Ask speakers, sponsors, and affiliates to all use the hashtag as they announce their participation.

During the event, it is a good idea to have somebody on your team monitor social media and share posts on the social networks, ensuring that each one includes the hashtag.

Drive interaction at your virtual event

"I've always been a big fan of hashtags at live events and it turns out virtual events are no different," said Stephanie Baiocchi, the director of community and events at IMPACT, a company is focused on empowering digital sales and marketing professionals and business leaders with the education, tools, training, and support needed to grow their companies and careers. "Hashtags, especially on Twitter and Instagram, are a way for attendees to connect and share how they're experiencing the event in a way that most virtual event platforms just aren't capable of doing. The stream of posts on an event's hashtag becomes sort of a virtual hallway where people can chat between sessions and share things they've learned with others. It's a bit more casual and organic than saying something in the chat section of a session."

In mid-March 2020, Baiocchi and the team at IMPACT made the call to postpone their in-person event, Digital Sales & Marketing World, which was scheduled for April 6th. They had so much great content that they did not want to wait to share it with their audience, nor did they want to leave them hanging. Instead, they decided to host a one-day virtual event instead.

"In about three weeks we managed to pull together this entire virtual event which ended up drawing over 3,000 registrants," Baiocchi said. "Granted, we already had most of the speakers lined up which was a huge part of why we were able to turn it around this quickly. However, there was still a lot to do in those few weeks. We had to find a platform and build out our entire event, test everything, and get all the necessary links to join into the virtual hands of our attendees."

The one-day virtual event, Digital Sales & Marketing Day, was a huge success for IMPACT, so much so that they did it again less than two months later with all new content. Soon they developed an ongoing program of virtual events.

"IMPACT's virtual events brought our audience together in a time of crushing isolation of quarantine," said Baiocchi. "Through our virtual events we were able to help businesses focus on the right things to weather the storm of the pandemic as much as possible and empower digital sales and marketing professionals to better connect, build trust, and sell virtually."

David was a speaker at IMPACT's April 6 Digital Sales & Marketing Day. Like all sessions that day, David's was prerecorded which allowed him to participate in the chat, live, as the recorded talk was playing. He answered questions, provided color commentary and connected personally with some audience members who had specific questions.

"To me, part of the magic of in-person events was always the human connection," Baiocchi said. "I know people feared losing this in the virtual space but if we have the technology available to connect with other attendees in real time just like at an in-person event and hashtags are a huge part of making that happen."

Another specific benefit of using a social media hashtag for event organizers is the ability to get a real-time pulse on how attendees feel about your event. "On the day of Digital Sales & Marketing Day, our first virtual event, I was a nervous wreck," Baiocchi said. "Between troubleshooting technical issues, managing a team responding to attendee questions, and co-hosting a live session, I felt like I had stepped outside of my body and was watching myself navigate this new virtual experience. However, a quick look at #DSMD2020 on Twitter showed me we were doing things right. Attendees were posting photos of their laptops shouting out the speakers they were enjoying. Some posted photos of dogs or cats next to their computers as they attended the event. But probably most satisfying was seeing our speakers connect with attendees just like they would at an in-person event and even seeing attendees connect with each other."

Baiocchi actively encourages attendees to share their experience on social media during the event. She is like a warm homeroom teacher putting the unruly kids into virtual groups and encouraging them to use their words to share what they are thinking. "I ask questions to get people to open up," she said. "Are you watching this while you make soup? Send me a picture on Twitter (and possibly the recipe too)! Is your kid right next to you e-learning and this is an opportunity for you to show them that you're a lifelong learner? I'd love to see that photo, plus you can connect with other parents attending the event who are also balancing work and parenting and e-learning."

The IMPACT virtual event program has benefitted the company in several important ways. The events allow them to continue their mission of educating their audience and empowering them to grow their businesses. Teaching through virtual events allows them to build trust with attendees which Baiocchi says definitely leads to some of them wanting to work with the company and use their services. Importantly, the virtual event programs have generated revenue which Baiocchi says has seriously helped their business during this challenging time.

Perhaps best of all for IMPACT is they have built a Fanocracy. Attendees at their virtual events are sharing and engaging and eager to participate in the next one. They are not just past or present attendees. They are fans of the company.

CHAPTER 4

Six Key Benefits to Hosting Virtual Events

Business events have been a staple in company calendars for hundreds of years — longer if we trace them back to Middle Eastern bazaars.

Nowadays, a few times a year, employees get to travel to places like Boston, New York, London, Las Vegas and Singapore to hear keynotes from world-renowned speakers, meet other like-minded professionals and enjoy entertainment. However, virtual events open the door for more people to attend more events than ever before.

Even as marketing has become more and more digital, in-person events have remained a mainstay in marketing budgets — then Covid-19 happened.

Every major event in 2020 took a year off or went virtual. Apple, SAP, Microsoft, Salesforce, Starbucks and Google are among the companies that opted to go online. Media brands like The Financial Times, TIME, The Atlantic, and Bloomberg transitioned their events from in-person to digital. Events including Shanghai

Fashion Week, The Aspen Ideas Festival, and even the Democratic and Republican National Conventions went virtual for the first time ever.

While it may seem like these were one-off moves in the face of a global pandemic, the reality is that the events scene may never be the same again. Virtual events are here to stay even when we get back to in-person events, and that is not a bad thing. What we are learning is that the benefits of virtual events for both attendees and hosts have the potential to permanently, and positively, change the event marketing landscape.

As compared with their offline counterparts, virtual evens can drive up attendance, help keep the budget under control, and improve the marketing strategy for future events. Even as in-person events slowly return, the clear advantages of virtual events, as well as the potential for a hybrid model, should have marketers re-thinking how they approach event marketing in the years to come.

In this chapter, we will look at six benefits of creating a virtual event:

1. Build fans of your business
2. Reach massive audiences
3. Save time for attendees and speakers
4. Save money
5. Create unique, online experiences
6. Get better event feedback

Build fans of your business

In Chapter 1, we touched on some ideas from David's book *Fanocracy: Turning Fans into Customers and Customers into Fans.* Essentially, humans are hardwired to want to be part of a tribe of like-minded people because that is where we feel safe and comfortable. When you create powerful virtual event, there are many possibilities to nurture an existing tribe or form a new one.

Surprisingly, a virtual event can be more intimate than an in-person event because of mirror neurons, the way our brains react to seeing video of people, which is covered in detail in Chapter 1. If a virtual event speaker looks directly at the camera and the image is cropped as if the speaker appears to be about four feet away from the audience, participants feel as if the speaker is talking directly to them.

It is surprising (but true) that a virtual event can feel warmer and intimate than an in-person one because each audience member feels as if the speakers are talking directly to them. Their mirror neurons are kicking in to tell them that they know the speakers personally even though intellectually they know they have not met in-person.

David experienced that hum when he spoke at the first virtual edition of Tony Robbins Business Mastery Seminar. Because he was able to speak directly to the cameras for most of his talk, people felt he was having a conversation with them, as opposed to being part of an audience of several thousand, which is the case when he is speaking at the in-person version of the event.

Fandom is also created at virtual events when people interact with speakers and with each other on social media and in the event app. This connection is formed when people come together to learn and share ideas. The best part of this is that the creation of this tribe of fans is a result of your event. And that can benefit your business for years to come.

Reach massive audiences

Saastr, one of the premier business conferences for the tech industry, generally welcomed about 10,000 in-person attendees. However, Saastr's first-ever virtual event in 2020 had 50,000 attendees registered. This is the power of hosting events online.

Physical events have physical limitations including square footage, seating capacity and venue availability, not to mention the costs of each attendee travelling to the event and paying for a hotel. Assuming your technology is capable of handling the volume, virtual events have no such limitations. Attendees do not need to plan or pay for travel. They also lose less time out of the office, so they can find time and budget to attend more events. As long as attendees can connect to the internet, then they can access an online event. This means your event can reach untold numbers of people from all over the world.

Events build brand awareness and give customers opportunities to learn, grow, and meet others. All these things can happen with a virtual event, but at a much larger scale. If your virtual experience is done right, you can mobilize your online audience into loyal brand fans from all parts of the globe.

Even after in-person events resume, offering a live streaming option, a hybrid combination of virtual and in-person, and recording keynotes and sessions to share later will be a way to tap into audiences far larger than any conference venue or stadium could hold.

Save time for attendees and speakers

If you have ever attended an out-of-state or out-of-country event, then you are familiar with hectic travel routines. Waking up early to catch a bus, train, or flight, checking into the hotel, navigating your way to the venue, registering, and finding the way to the room you want to be — the time associated with just making it to an event can be enough to discourage people from attending at all. The added cost of time and money for attendees can make an event a no-go, but a virtual event a can-do.

With virtual events, the only hassle for attendees is making sure they have a good internet connection. With everything just a few clicks away, people can enjoy the benefits of events without having to lose valuable time and money to travel.

For event planners, booking speakers becomes more flexible as well. Speakers find themselves booked out for events all across the globe, making it hard to squeeze in last-minute requests or adjust schedules. We cannot be two places at once. But with virtual events, these constraints are minimized.

With virtual events, speakers can deliver content from a home studio. While speakers need to tailor their talks to create a unique experience specifically for the online medium, the added time of travel does not need to be a part of pre-speech preparation anymore, and there is no need to decline that event in Dublin because you are already booked in Dubai.

Save money

According to event software provider Bizzabo, businesses spent nearly a quarter of their marketing budget on events in 2019. Some of the costs for in-person events include booking a venue, securing a roster of speakers, paying event staff, food and beverage, producing signs and physical branding, and creating unique experiences for attendees.

This does not account for event management software, event apps, and promotional expenses. Maybe your company has a budget for these things, but there is no denying the high cost of producing an in-person event.

With a virtual event, physical event costs disappear. Notably, the venue booking costs no longer eat a massive chunk of the budget. With some major concert venues (where large-scale business events also take place) costing as much as $500,000 per day, event planners can now put those dollars to use towards other parts of the event or other business initiatives.

On the attendee side, ticket fees can drop markedly. The all-access pass for HubSpot's INBOUND 2019 stood at $799; the same pass for the digital INBOUND 2020 is currently available $69. On top of that, the general pass for INBOUND 2020 is completely free. Other virtual events are experimenting with a tiered approach as well, allowing them to bring in would-be fans at a free level, but offer their diehard fanbase premium experiences that are well worth the price tag.

Now, this is not to say that virtual events are cost-free, and we dig into the costs in detail in Chapter 8. To run a great virtual event, you will want to have more than your laptop webcam and a free Zoom account. While the free Zoom option is great for small meetings, it is limited to up to 100 participants and a 40-minute maximum for groups. And even for a recurring webinar series, you will want to ensure that your hosts have good lighting and sound.

For a large-scale event, costs will include the hosting platform, app development, payment and attendee management software, developer or other technical fees, speaker fees, production fees, etc. You may also be considering swag, premium attendee enhancements, and other add-ons that will carry a price tag. (See Chapter 8 for details.)

However, there is no doubt that on a per-attendee basis, it is much less expensive to host a virtual event than an in-person one. Those lower costs can be passed on to attendees in the form of lower ticket prices, be invested in enhancing the virtual experience and appeal, or contribute to your bottom line.

Create unique, online experiences

Physical events bring to mind sitting in a ballroom or auditorium to hear a speech, wandering through trade booths where workers hand out swag, chatting in line for the buffet and meeting up with fellow professionals over a coffee or a glass of wine. While virtual events cannot replicate these things, they can offer unique experiences that change how we think of events.

When David keynoted the Skillsoft Perspectives 2020 summit (discussed in Chapter 2), which was originally planned as a series of separate regional events across multiple continents, the event planners reimagined the series into one online event for a global audience. Attendees could tune in based on their time zone and were treated to top-notch content from speakers over 24 hours including 97 pre-recorded case studies, product sessions, and presentations. More than 14,000 attendees participated.

Attendees enjoyed interacting with speakers, each other, and employees of Skillsoft. They did so within the event app and on social media via the #perspectives2020 hashtag, which had 2,700 social media interactions across the various platforms (Twitter in particular) during the 24-hour event, as participants discussed what was happening.

Apps and social media integrations can be effective for increasing the vibrancy of interactions at any event. For a virtual event, tools like these will play a critical role for networking and engagement. Something as simple as LinkedIn integration into a matchmaking or other networking tool can allow fleeting digital connections to take on lasting significance.

Event hosts can work with sponsors to produce morning coffee gatherings where they recap the highlights from the previous day. Sponsors might host a premium dinner party where everyone makes a recipe together and then enjoys it over a glass of wine in a virtual gathering. Virtual events also offer an opportunity to rethink the "swag problem" in which tons of stress balls end up in hotel waste baskets every year. Instead, branded coffee mugs, the keynote speaker's latest book, and even dinner fixings delivered to an attendee's doorstep offer an ideal opportunity for social sharing and extended marketing. Fans care. Fans share.

One truly innovative example of a virtual event taking things to a new level is the incorporation of concerts into Fortnite. A massive digital avatar of the rapper Travis Scott gave a performance of hit songs in May 2020, with the game environment shifting to give players an immersive experience full of special effects and new landscapes to explore. The game's concert had over 12 million online attendees, making it one of the most-attended events in world history. Given this event's success, Fortnight launched a concert series with the goal of making Fortnight a standard stop on bands' tour schedules.

Online events that optimize for the digital medium give attendees something unique that can only happen virtually. When done right, these events can attract and delight millions of people from all over the globe.

Get better event feedback

Any event planner worth their salt wants to gather feedback about their event. They should be asking attendees what worked well, which speakers rocked the crowd, and what could be better for next time.

For an in-person event, organizers might gather feedback through an event app, though most likely they will tally up a net promoter score based upon an email sent to attendees a few days after the event. The reality, however, is that it can be tough to gather meaningful information from attendees. In the moment, they are busy learning from speakers, entertainers, and like-minded peers. After the event, they have moved back into the routine of work and life and just do not take the time to provide feedback.

With an online event, attendees will be on screens for the entire time. With the right event management software, you can send in-event engagement surveys and collect feedback immediately after an event, or even at the individual session level. You can also very easily see how many people attended certain online sessions and which speakers seemed to get the most engagement from the audience beyond the old crowd volume test.

Digital offers other interaction. Think heart and !!! emojis. If organizers enable real time reactions and ratings, which are monitored during and analyzed after an event, they can learn a great deal — maybe more than from post-event surveys. With social media integration (and monitoring), real-time chat and attendee comments, organizers have the opportunity to gain unprecedented audience insights that go well beyond standard satisfaction surveys.

CHAPTER 5

Format, Features and Platform Considerations

Producing a virtual event requires wrangling many different people, technologies, and ideas. There are a number of critical elements you will need to consider, which depend on many factors including objectives, budget, size, complexity and more. Each event, like each fandom, has unique elements that must be considered to satisfy a particular audience. This guide is not all-inclusive, but should provide a solid framework for evaluating your needs.

Technology to host a virtual event

Given that you are moving your event online, the technology component will be one of the first things you must consider. Some organizations will build from the ground up, but most will look for purpose built or existing solutions to use out of the box or customize.

Webinar software for basic events

If you are hosting a basic event where you're not charging a registration fee in the platform, you might consider webinar platforms such as Microsoft Teams, Zoom, or GoToWebinar. You might be familiar with these companies' tools for collaboration or meetings. However, webinar software from these types of online meeting companies differ a bit from the base platforms many people use to meet with colleagues.

At its core, webinar software is a fairly straightforward one-to-many solution. It allows a presentation to be shown and, generally, an image of the presenter to appear alongside it. Many of us are familiar with the basic free-to-attend webinar.

As you evaluate the options out there, some features you want to consider are administrative controls such as muting and unmuting panelists, selective recording of the event, Q&A moderation, polling, breakout rooms, registration, reporting and so on.

You will want to consider the ability to customize the setting (branding), as well as the ability to optimize the presentation. For example, you may want the speaker's slides to appear in a specific part of the screen. You may want to set a default view for attendees. The tool might satisfy you out of the box. Just know that not every platform provides customization of the presentation layer.

Most webinar platforms are not optimized for interaction. They are designed, essentially, to broadcast information. However, you will want to understand exactly what you can do in this context and whether the tool allows you to provide the level of community and interaction that is appropriate for your audience.

Some webinar platforms include the ability to live stream to social sites like Facebook Live and YouTube (a few even include

LinkedIn). Social integration can increase engagement and feedback, so this is worth considering as a lower cost way to provide interactivity as well as to increase the reach of your webinar.

Integrated platforms for larger events

To provide a much more integrated approach for a virtual event, similar to larger in-person events, you may need a virtual event platform. You will also want to consider a virtual event platform if you are going to charge admission to your online event.

There are dozens of virtual event platforms. Some that we have used include BigMarker, Bizzabo, INXPO, ON24, and Cvent, as well as custom-built platforms.

Virtual event platforms offer a wide variety of features and experiences such as multiple presentation tracks, roundtable discussions, a virtual tradeshow, breakout rooms, virtual press conferences, networking, and more.

The multiple presentation track feature, for example, allows for several simultaneous presentations to happen at one time so that attendees can choose the one that is best for them. These can be presented live, recorded in advance, or a combination of the two.

Some platforms also have either their own smartphone app or seamless links to a partner app where participants can manage registration, connect with others, and more. Note that an app allows the organizer to better control the experience and may facilitate networking. However, it may also inhibit virtual attendees who want to multitask during an event.

Interestingly, some virtual event platforms work seamlessly with webinar platforms like Zoom. The best way to think of this approach is that the presenters use Zoom with the resulting feed (or recorded talk) delivered to the virtual event platform where participants view the presentations. Using this approach, the virtual event platform handles attendee user interface, registration, permissions, credit card fees, and so on.

Registration and participation management

If you are hosting a simple webinar, the platform you choose can be used to register people to attend.

However, if you are running a larger event with multiple tracks, an event where people come and go over hours or days, and/or a paid event, you will need more. These events are much more complex and require software to process credit card payments and manage people's credentials to be able to see the content. You will also likely want a solution that integrates with your existing CRM and analytics tools.

You will need to manage the customer throughout the sales process, throughout the event, and afterwards. Thus, when you are evaluating platforms, be sure to identify all of the aspects that will touch the attendees and sponsors. You want to optimize the entire experience for these key stakeholders, and, of course, you want to ensure that any new customers become lasting ones.

Key considerations as you evaluate platforms for your large virtual event

As a professional keynote speaker and virtual event speaker, David has presented using a dozen or so virtual event platforms. As a presenter, moderator, interviewer and event organizer, Michelle has tested and worked with about a dozen as well. They each have pros and cons that are way beyond the scope of this book.

However, the one aspect that is extremely limiting is when the platform is hardcoded so that presenters' slides are way bigger than the video stream of the presenter.

You want to be sure that the virtual event audience can see the speakers, particularly in the case of marquee names and featured keynotes. That may sound obvious, but many digital presentation platforms make the presentation slides big and the speaker tiny, with no options to modify the view.

As you are evaluating platforms, make sure that you have the ability to show the speaker in full screen and the speaker can present without the platform's slide presentation feature. Audiences tend to get bored with big slides and a tiny video and many won't stick around for an entire presentation, much less hours of them. Remember: Humans connect with humans, even virtually. Being able to control this presentation layer will be a critical differentiator for event producers.

If you want a fabulous event, you need to make your presenters look fabulous. Unfortunately, the vast majority of presenters at virtual events will simply set up their notebook computer (or worse, their smartphone) on a table and present. The lighting, sound, camera angle, etc. can, unfortunately, be of poor quality. (Helping your presenters shine is an absolutely essential component of producing a successful virtual event and we will cover it in more detail in the next chapter.)

Don't overlook the technology required for the presenters. You may need to insist that speakers have, at a minimum, a good webcam, a good microphone, some lighting, and a way to raise the camera so it is at eye level (a stack of books work great for this).

You should perform a technology check with speakers prior to the event to make sure they are presenting well. Most in-person events provide speaker guidelines and prep calls. Your virtual event should be held to at least the same standard. After all, making your speakers look good makes you look good too.

Pre-recorded vs. live

Most webinar and event platforms allow for either a live virtual presentation or the ability to play a pre-recorded presentation. There are pros and cons to each approach, so you will want to consider which one is best for your event.

When you pre-record a virtual presentation, you can eliminate many of the technical issues that can plague a live session.

Your speakers may be more comfortable presenting in a recorded format because if they make a mistake they can go back and re-record all or part of the talk and talks can often be edited. While a professional speaker will not have any issues with live vs. pre-recorded from a delivery standpoint, speakers who do not have much experience (such as company executives or sponsors of your event) may be nervous and prefer the ability to go back and re-record.

There is always the potential for making mistakes as a speaker works a feature such as playing a video or transitioning to live Q&A. In addition, some experienced speakers may be uncomfortable with the virtual presentation technology you are using.

Pre-recording a session also helps to eliminate the possibility of Wi-Fi or other issues at a speaker's location messing up the talk. David has given several hundred talks from his home studio. Michelle has produced or participated in countless remote sessions as well. While nearly all have been free of technical difficulties, we've both experienced a few.

Once, the power went out during David's talk. He delivered it via mobile phone while the producer drove his slides. It wasn't ideal, but it worked. Another time, a neighbor chose the precise moment of one of his presentations to remove a tree. Cutting it down wasn't a big deal but wow was it noisy when the tree was shoved into the grinder that turned it into wood chips. Michelle suffered an internet outage while hosting an event, but by design had designated a backup host to take over — which went smoothly. Pre-recording would have eliminating these issues.

Of particular challenge with pre-recorded sessions is speaker interaction. One way to handle this is to ask attendees to send in questions ahead of time. Another is to follow up a recorded session with a shorter live Q&A, which can be held on the organizer's platform or via social media.

However, an added benefit of pre-recorded sessions is that they provide fodder for marketing the event or specific sessions before and during the event. Soundbites and video clips provide excellent tools for giving potential attendees a taste of why an event is worth the ticket price, or to help them decide between enticing alternatives. For sponsors, small "commercials" can be run as interstitials during an event, which increases exposure and the value of their sponsorship.

Presenting live is great because a speaker can build in interactive elements into the talk. Using features built into the platforms such as chat, reactions, polling, and Q&A allow for the audience and the speaker to interact in real-time.

Live content also creates incentive to be present during the actual event in order to interact with fellow audience members and speakers and be "part of the conversation."

We recommend that, whenever possible, you should go with a live presentation or, at minimum, incorporate live elements into your events. The ability to engage with the audience via chat, polling, and other interactive tools is very powerful.

One way to build a totally interactive live experience together with the safety of pre-recording is to pre-record a backup version of the talk, which is ready to play in case of any technical issues. A speaker will record their talk a week or so before the event, which the event producer has queued up and ready to play in case of issues. Then, when the live talk is happening, the production team will play the video in parallel to the live talk so if it is needed, they can switch to the recording. Suggestion: If you go this route, have the speaker wear the same outfit for pre-recording and live so a potential transition mid-talk is less jarring to the audience.

If you use this approach, we suggest that the producer makes an announcement of what's happening so the audience understands the nature of the technical problem. Sometimes, even with connectivity issues, it is still possible to do Q&A via the speaker's mobile phone.

If you can not pre-record a backup, ensure that the organizer has a copy of the speaker's presentation and a way to dial in by phone in case they are unable to maintain a connection or sufficient bandwidth to perform their talk as originally planned. To paraphrase Louis Pasteur, "Luck favors the prepared."

For many organizers, a model that incorporates live and pre-recorded content will offer the best of both: dynamic, must-see events along with polished, professional presentations. It is critical to consider ways in which engagement can be achieved around pre-recorded segments, of course, and to offer live segments that will coalesce an audience and build a shared, tribal experience.

Should you offer a replay of the sessions?

Traditional old-school webinars almost always have the ability for people to either participate live or watch the recording of the session at their convenience. While it is nice for people to be able to watch at a later date, the problem is that fewer people will participate live and the potential for interaction is reduced.

In addition, there are many people who sign up for a virtual event and don't bother to attend, knowing that they can watch later. However, many people with good intentions simply will not tune in after the fact. We have seen the percentage of people who actually attend a live virtual event versus how many register steadily decline over the past year or so. Now, it is not uncommon for only 30 or 40 percent of people who register to actually attend.

There are several ways to build your event to entice as many people as possible to participate live.

Some virtual events are now organized around a strict "no replay" format. If you don't watch live, you are out of luck. Other events permit a subset of sessions to be replayed. For example, keynotes can be watched later but panel discussions and product demonstrations must be attended live.

An interesting hybrid model is also used by some virtual events. The live virtual event is one price and all the sessions are live. Later, the sessions are available as a replay but that requires an additional charge.

In some cases, there is a tiered approach to this kind of hybrid pricing that might look something like having the live sessions priced at one level, say $200, while live plus replays are another price, say $250. In this model, replays are only available after the event for the same price of $250. Pricing in this way offers the benefits of the replays but an incentive to watch live.

The variables of platform features, format, and production are vast. While that can seem daunting, it means that you have the opportunity and ability to customize to suit your audience. Dig in, explore what's out there and align it with your objectives. And don't be afraid to change directions or expectations as your experience with virtual events matures and evolves.

CHAPTER 6

Speaker Preparation for Virtual Events

Event organizers have a difficult job. Many are trying to figure out how to bring formerly in-person events online. But more than that, they need to rethink what is possible with a virtual event to experience true success.

Over the years, many event organizers have shared with us that the toughest part of the job is ensuring that the event will have excellent speakers. They must ensure diversity among the speakers, including that of race and gender. It also means thinking about including diverse perspectives, which will come from a wide range of backgrounds, experiences, and industries. They must find compelling speakers who are representative of, reflective of, and also aspirational and inspirational for their intended audience.

Then it all comes down to choosing someone with something to say who can say it well. For virtual events, it is even more difficult because most in-person speakers are not experienced with this setting or the skill set required to navigate it successfully.

Speakers skilled in virtual events can make your event great.

It does not make sense to invest time and money into your virtual event only to have your attendees disappointed because the speakers you choose do not have much experience presenting on virtual events. Content, and the speakers that deliver it, are critical for your event's success.

Speakers include experienced keynoters, stand-alone session speakers, expert panelists, sponsor speakers, C-level or celebrity speakers, panel moderators, skilled interviewers, and more. You likely have a variety of channels for speaker recruiting, including speaker bureaus, authors of hot new industry books and other marquee names, industry experts, academics and journalists. Unfortunately, while many of them might shine at an in-person event, not all have perfected the skill of virtual presentations.

At one event David worked on, a well-known speaker who charges about $50,000 for an in-person talk was also on the program. Now, he may not have charged that for the virtual event, but at any price, his virtual presentation skills were terrible. He presented on his smartphone in portrait mode with the phone held down low so that it was pointed up his nose and to the lights in the ceiling of his office. Being an experienced speaker is not enough; it is critical employ speakers who have mastered the art of the virtual presentation and understand the differences between the needs of presenting virtually and in person.

How different is it to give a speech virtually versus face-to-face?

As discussed in detail in Chapter 2, many organizations shifting from in-person to virtual events simply try to recreate what they know to the digital world. Unfortunately, they fail to find the right toolset for virtual success because virtual events are more like television than theater. This has powerful ramifications for speakers.

"In virtual events, you don't get much back from the audience, and it demands more emotion and variety from a presenter than face-to-face speaking," said Dr. Nick Morgan. Morgan is David's long-time speaker coach, President of Public Words Inc. and author, most recently, of *Can You Hear Me? How to Connect with People in a Virtual World*, published by Harvard in 2018. "You need to amp up your emotional energy, gesture more and make sure the audience can see your gestures."

It seems counter-intuitive to many speakers that when delivering a talk to the small screen of virtual events, they need to gesture more than when they are on a large stage playing to thousands of people.

Morgan, who has studied this for years, says the importance of focusing on emotional energy is related to how we look on a screen. "Video crushes people, who are three-dimensional, into two dimensions," he said. "That means our faces — and the expressions on our faces — are flattened. If you've got great cheekbones, first of all, lucky you. Second, that helps make your face look good and be expressive in two dimensions. But for the rest of us, our emotions and reactions are subtly lessened by being on video."

On a large in-person stage, experienced speakers use gestures frequently to convey unspoken ideas to the audience. Having wide open arms, for example, shows an audience that a speaker is warm and open and welcoming. However, those big moves that work so well on a stage or in a hotel ballroom don't always work for a speaker appearing on a screen. It is simple logistics; as speakers, we need to be conscious of the "box" that is visible to the audience and be aware that your arms in that wide-open stance aren't even showing up on the screen because the shot is from your chest. Gesture frequently, but tight enough to be seen.

"A speaker needs to make it clear what he or she cares about," Morgan added. "That's one of the ways audiences pay attention to speakers: What does he or she think is most important here? Don't let the attitude go unspoken."

Five common problems with virtual event speakers

As you evaluate speakers, consider these problems. Professional speakers should already be prepared to deliver a top-notch talk. That is why they get paid to speak, so they should already have the skills down. But you will need to check to be sure. Meanwhile, you will also need to work with other speakers who don't have as much experience.

We have identified five of the common problems in hiring

virtual event speakers that can sink your virtual event.

Speakers who are skilled at in-person events may not be skilled virtual speakers

Delivering an awesome in-person talk requires drama. In-person events are a theatrical performance. It is a powerful and rare thing for a speaker to have several thousand people in a room paying attention to their every word and move.

Skilled in-person speakers understand audience interaction, knowing when a reaction will come, and how to make it work in the context of the overall talk. They are adept at using a big stage, making certain to visit the outer limits of the stage to mix things up. Perhaps they venture into the audience to engage directly with members of the crowd. They know from experience what the response to a well-rehearsed line or joke will be.

None of this is true at a virtual event. All of the familiar live cues are gone, and the speaker is left alone in a room staring at a camera.

The biggest difference is that virtual events are more like television shows than theatrical experiences. However, most in-person speakers simply try to recreate the in-person event they are familiar with. Instead of creating a powerful virtual talk, they default to the style that's worked for them in the past and film it.

Speakers must reimagine what is possible in a virtual world, planning their talks like a live television show. In fact, speakers who have television or one-way video experience like YouTube will be more adept at the virtual event format.

In Chapter 1, we discussed the neuroscience of fandom including the power of cropping video as if the audience member is within about four feet of a virtual speaker. Because of mirror neurons, our brain processes video cropped in this way as if we are in the same room as the speaker on camera even though intellectually, we know we are not. However, that is just the first step. Just as important is the ability to play to a camera, to connect via eye contact with the audience.

Surprisingly, a virtual event where speakers talk directly to the camera in a warm and casual tone can feel more intimate than an in-person event where the speaker is 30, 50, or even hundreds of feet away on a far-off stage. But it requires skill to look into that camera when every part of you wants to look at your slides, to peek at the attendee chat, or to check out at the video of participants.

In a virtual event, people's attention spans are much shorter than if people are gathered in a convention center or hotel ballroom. This means speakers need to mix things up, adding elements of surprise and visual interest. They also need to include the audience as much as possible.

As you evaluate virtual event speakers, make sure they are skilled at virtual events. Ask to see video of them in action at a recent virtual event, preferably one similar to what you are planning.

For example, if you are organizing a major event with speakers located in a professional studio, ask to see video shot in a studio. If you plan to have the speaker deliver the talk from their home, take a look at a video from an event where they presented from home. Ask about their experience with virtual events and for some of the tactics they use to keep audiences engaged.

A good way to evaluate and book a skilled speaker is to work with a speaker bureau, because the professionals at bureaus work to connect speakers with events. The same suggestions apply, however: You need to evaluate the speakers they suggest based on the ability to deliver a virtual talk. If you are not already working with a bureau, you can research them at the International Association of Speakers Bureaus website. IASB is the trade association for speaker bureaus and each company listed agrees to work with agreed promoting standards of excellence.

Virtual speakers may not have the right technology at home

Speakers who frequently present from a stage are not accustomed to setting up the technology for their presentation. They simply show up, have a conversation with the production team, and do a technology check to review aspects of the performance venue including staging, sound, lighting and video camera placement.

None of these details are up to the speaker. The host has planned for months and put a great deal of work into delivering a polished setting and professional quality environment.

Virtual speaking from speakers' homes is completely different. Every aspect of the technology is up to the speaker including the background, camera and microphone location, lighting, and much more. Sadly, most speakers do not focus enough on the technology and setting to create great virtual talks.

Many speakers simply set up their notebook computer on their dining table. Unfortunately, poor camera placement and less than ideal lighting reflects badly on both the speaker and the event itself.

An important consideration with hiring a virtual event speaker is the technical aspects of how they will present. Make sure you have an opportunity to evaluate a speaker's use of virtual speaking technology before you decide to hire them. David covers some of this in the six-minute video published to *Vimeo Virtual Events vs In-Person Events: How Do They Compare?*, which he shared earlier in this book.

If you are working with unpaid speakers, it is essential that you provide them with speaker and technology tips and guidelines. Here are a few things to include:

- **Background:** A simple background without clutter is best. If the speaker lives in a small apartment that doesn't have a suitable background, something like a Japanese shoji screen, or a white wall can be a good compromise. Tell them not to use a virtual background (more on this later).

- **Camera placement:** It is best when the camera is positioned at eye-level to the speaker, producing an image that to the audience looks about four feet away. Ideally, a good quality webcam should be used.

- **Lighting:** Never position a speaker with windows or bright lights behind them. Their face should always be lit either by natural light or you can suggest that they purchase a small ring light.

- **Microphone:** Ideally, an external microphone like the Yeti model made by Blue Microphones should be used. Relying on the mic that is built into a computer can deliver poor quality sound, or worse, generate feedback. And speakers should be discouraged from using in ear headphone/mic combinations, because of poor quality sound.

- **Headphones:** Any headphones will look less than ideal on camera. However, they do have a distinct benefit for speakers because they don't cause feedback like using computer sound can. Wireless Bluetooth headphones don't have unsightly cords, but can potentially cause problems with other devices, such as a microphone, and result in muffled sound.

It is ideal to do a brief test with every speaker prior to the day of filming or of the live event. This way, the event producers can troubleshoot camera angles, background, sound, lighting, etc.

Virtual speakers might not involve the audience in their presentation

The challenge for online events is to develop the community that in-person events naturally create. As discussed in Chapter 3, through the native tools built into virtual event platforms, attendees can chat with one another, live. After a talk, virtual meeting rooms help people who share common goals can collaborate based on the information they just learned.

The big problem is that most virtual event speakers who simply try to recreate the stage experience from a physical event don't have experience with virtual audience interaction. They are unfamiliar with how to use online tools to develop interaction between people in real time. A lack of interaction during such talks means the one-way nature of the delivery can be boring for the audience because it's no different than a YouTube video of a speech.

There are several ways to get the audience involved in a virtual presentation. Most virtual event platforms have interactive tools including chat, polling, Q&A, and breakout rooms.

Ask the speaker you are considering hiring for your virtual event if they have ways of building audience interaction into their talks. If a virtual event speaker is skilled at capitalizing on the unique features of the virtual event platform, there is a powerful transformation from a one-way delivery of content into an interactive experience involving each audience member.

Again: It is the event organizer's job to prepare speakers who are not experienced with presenting virtually. Familiarize them with the tools available in your platform. For any speaker, the organizer or producer should be ready to offer suggestions on how to increase engagement and interaction, tell them what tools are at their disposal, and then help them figure out ways in which they will engage the audience.

Virtual event speakers don't forge a true partnership with event planners

There are many aspects of presenting at a virtual event that go beyond the actual talk. A virtual event speaker needs to be prepared to respond to requests quickly, participate in a technology rehearsal, and, of course, understand the event and its audience to hone their talk.

Those are the basics, though. A true virtual event speaker partnership with an event goes much further.

For example, a virtual event speaker who creates a short promotional video for the event to use on their site to generate registration is being a good partner.

A virtual event speaker who promotes their appearance on their social media feeds is being a good partner.

A virtual event speaker who offers something "extra" such as a private Q&A with VIP clients, or a few complimentary signed copies of their latest book to the event as a giveaway is being a good partner.

Many events have active social media backchannels. An event hashtag is very effective leading up to an event, and to provide an interactive channel (and real-time feedback) during an event, as we shared in Chapter 3. Some events integrate social feeds into their apps, recognizing that this is a fundamental way in which people interact.

These strategies move the content from a one-way conversation (think TED talk) to an interactive conversation (people in the audience discussing the speaker's topic which brings in their networks around the world). A virtual event speaker who is a true partner will be active in the social backchannel before and after their talk.

Event managers should feel comfortable asking about what a speaker will bring to the table. There are many ways that a speaker can add extra value, and a good virtual event speaker partner will be happy to offer suggestions of how they can help make your event great.

Virtual backgrounds are bad for your event's brand

Northern Lights? A beach with waves and the wind in a palm tree? Your logo? If you want to be taken seriously, use a real background. Fake virtual backgrounds are cheesy. This is even more true for larger virtual events. Image matters.

Besides the tacky nature of virtual backgrounds, there's also the problem with the "ghosting" effect that happens when a speaker moves. For a split second the virtual background disappears, and you can see the room behind. David demonstrated this in a silly video he posted on LinkedIn: *Zoom Virtual Backgrounds Are Terrible For Your Brand*.

A speaker's personal brand is important. You are sharing a piece of yourself via every channel that you communicate on. The novelty of a virtual background might be funny on a Zoom call with your team, but it is not the image a polished speaker (or event) wants to put forth. In fact, they almost always pixelate and create artifacts around the speaker that are distracting at best and disastrous at worst.

Sure, your room might be a little messy. And your cat may make an unexpected appearance. It happens.

But the most important thing for is to be real. Speakers: Use a real background, even if it is just a wall behind you. Event organizers: be sure that you help your speakers optimize their background, lighting, camera angle, and set up. While not everyone has a virtual studio, most of us can identify a good spot in the house and move the ironing board or exercise bike out of the shot.

The importance of a production team

Every virtual event, even smaller ones hosted on Zoom or a similar platform, should have a skilled team behind the scenes facilitating the technology so speakers can focus on presenting. The larger and more involved the virtual event is, the more important the production team becomes.

When David presented at Tony Robbins Business Mastery from Tony's purpose-built virtual event studio in Florida, there were nearly 30 people working behind the scenes to make his talk, and the other presentations over the five days, as dynamic as possible. With a large event like the virtual Business Mastery, there might be several people working sound, three to five camera operators, technical directors, production management, people who coordinate special guests, a stage manager, and a dozen or more people to manage how the resulting live feed is fed to participants.

When David was on the Business Mastery virtual stage, he focused one hundred percent on delivering the best talk he could because he was comfortable knowing that all the backstage details were professionally taken care of. David's videos would roll when required, his virtual guests would be on the screen ready for David to speak with at the right moment, his music was queued and ready to go when it was time to play them, and the audience was able to interact with the program live.

The same thing is true with smaller events.

When you are hosting several hundred people on a platform like Zoom, you should still plan on having a person or several people working the technology so the speaker can focus on presenting. On small DCN events, Michelle works with a team of four who manage everything from session content to speaker guidance, production, technical issues, and optimal recording. Every session has a technology run through several days before the live event airs to run through expectations with the speaker(s), prepare for any potential issues with a backup plan, and help speakers optimize for the toolset available.

How speakers and producers work together to make an event great

At virtual events produced by The Growth Faculty, organizers pay very close attention to the back end production in order to make the audience experience as powerful as possible.

Over more than a decade, The Growth Faculty has produced in-person events in Australia, New Zealand, and Singapore, bringing such leaders as Hillary Clinton, Barack and Michelle Obama, Malcolm Gladwell and Simon Sinek to the Asia-Pacific region. When the pandemic shut down in-person events, The Growth Faculty pivoted to a virtual Masterclass with Global Thought Leaders series, 90-minute sessions with bestselling authors and thought leaders from around the world. David presented at one in September 2020, delivering a session on the Zoom webinar platform titled *Turning Customers to Fans in Challenging Times*. It was a delight for David to focus on his presentation, knowing the technology was being taken care of behind the scenes.

"Our virtual Masterclass with Global Thought Leaders series has become even more important during these COVID times when businesses and teams have had to innovate, adapt to new ways of working as well as find new ways to create value for their customers," said Karen Beattie, founder and head of strategy at The Growth Faculty. "We ensure that our presenters are fully briefed and supported through the entire event planning process so when they turn on up the day of the virtual meeting, they are confident we know what we are doing, and they can focus on their presentation."

As a speaker, David particularly likes a detailed technology check about a week before a live virtual event so he can virtually meet the production team, test the platform, work out the timeline for such things as polling, chat, breakouts, videos, and guest interviews as well as plan for disruptions such as internet connectivity issues.

"We had to learn how to host effective virtual meeting fast and we transferred the level of detail from our in-person event management checklists across to the virtual platform," Beattie said. "It took what seemed an extraordinary amount of time in preparation, as we were learning and creating new processes for our virtual meetings."

The preparation work going into a 90-minute talk can easily take five or ten times as long as the presentation will run, but the pre-event work is important to make sure everything is planned for.

"Our team would run rehearsal meetings to test the various functions on Zoom," Beattie said. "We usually set up a briefing call with each speaker to ensure we cater for their specific presentation needs. What people miss most about the live events is the interaction with other attendees, so we are always looking for ways to facilitate this effectively in a virtual environment. Connection with other delegates online is important and our masterclasses are 90 minutes in length. We allow 60 minutes for content and 30 minutes for interaction through Q & A or break out rooms. It creates a level of intimacy and our speakers seem to be very accessible in this environment."

Yes, David was proud of the content he presented — as any professional speaker should be. However, having the experience of working on many events reinforces how the production team at The Growth Faculty elevated his performance and the audience experience.

Provide your speakers with guidelines and guidance

Every event is different. Every audience is different. As the organizer, you are best equipped to understand the appropriate tone for your speakers. For any event, you need to provide speakers with a good picture of who will be in the audience and what will best serve them. This is particularly critical for virtual events given that the speaker won't be able to see the audience and react to them live.

If speakers need to use a specific platform to record, provide them with download instructions and ask that they do it prior to your test session. Give them some idea of the toolset available or point them to further information about it. Most speakers want to do their best; empower them to do so.

You may need to provide speakers with specific video or software settings to ensure that all presentations are recorded at the same quality and with a similar view or set up.

While you may not be able to require that speakers have specific technology at their disposal, it is reasonable to make recommendations. This might include suggesting a good webcam, microphone and lighting.

It may sound obvious, but you will need to remind many virtual event speakers to ensure that they are on a stable internet connection, have shut down bandwidth-intensive programs, and have turned their phones to do not disturb.

You will also need to remind them to optimize their physical setting, which includes an appropriate background, letting others know they are recording, being in a quiet space, and ensuring that they are centered in the video frame.

Of particular importance is reminding speakers to make eye contact with the camera. You'll also want to ensure that the camera is as close to eye level as possible. If they are using a laptop, this may require elevating it.

Not every event has a dress code. But it is fine to let speakers know if there is one, or to remind them that the session is being recorded and delivered to hundreds, or thousands, of people and ask them to dress accordingly. Let them know to avoid stripes as they can cause strobing on many webcams.

Lighting can be a particular challenge for virtual speakers. Some will have a studio set up with terrific lighting. Others might have a simple ring light. Most will need to optimize based on what they've got on hand.

Encourage speakers to test their lighting prior to your prep session (or the event itself). Speakers should avoid backlight or filming outside or next to a window as a rule because it will cause them to appear washed out. Overhead lights can cause a shine on the top of the speaker's head. And when using a desk light, check for any hard shadows.

Helping your speakers look good will help them present more confidently. And it will ensure that your event content is polished and professional, which reflects well on your brand.

CHAPTER 7

The Business of Virtual Events

While events vary as much as the audiences they serve, there are several broad categories of virtual events that you may want to consider.

Types of virtual events

Basic webinars offered at no charge to participants

Webinars have been around for well more than a decade. In the old days, a webinar was simply a speaker talking over their slides for an hour or so. Later, the ability to have a small thumbnail video of the speaker became available as well as the ability to handle audience Q&A. These basic webinars are still around but benefit from significant advances in technology.

Webinars are a type of virtual events that are ideal if you want to provide thought leadership content as a way to generate interest in your ideas, products, or services. A webinar is also a great way to host a virtual event that can generate sales leads because those who choose to participate are likely be a good fit for the product or service your company sells.

Simple events where you charge a fee

Some virtual event organizers host a simple event, or series of sessions, with a one or several speakers and charge a fee for the event or for each session. While the same webinar platform can be used, this approach requires additional technology to accept payments.

An event where you charge a fee to participate is an ideal way for an organization or individual with specialized knowledge to monetize their expertise and ideas in new ways.

Larger events with multiple tracks

Many types of organizations host a much more integrated virtual event, similar to larger in-person events. These may take place over several days, can include dozens or even hundreds of speakers, and might have sponsors. A large event may be free for participants, a paid event, or a combination of the two.

For this kind of virtual event, you will need a platform that offers a wide variety of features that provide participant experiences such as multiple presentation tracks, roundtable discussions, a virtual tradeshow, breakout rooms, and much more. Simple webinar tools will not suffice.

A large event is ideal for organizations who are replacing their in-person client conference or tradeshow for the virtual world.

Pricing your Virtual Event

If you plan to charge people to attend your virtual event, you are in for a challenge.

With the move to virtual events in early 2020, pricing for attendees has varied widely. Some events that used to cost over $1,000 for an in-person ticket became totally free in a virtual setting. However, other events have kept pricing at same level as when the event was in-person. Still others are experimenting with tiered models, in which some content is free while other content is considered premium and requires a fee.

Start with your goals. Then take a look at competitive or similar events. Consider offering discount rates or free tickets to certain highly desirable audience segments or groups you particularly want to attract. The reality is that you will need to innovate on the value proposition for paid attendees and articulate it through your marketing. This is going to require some experimentation in price points and messaging, but know that people are paying to attend valuable virtual events.

Fully paid virtual event

For some organizations, a paid event makes the most sense (often because it is the organization's primary source of revenue or a critical revenue stream). These events might be large or small. However, no matter what the size, they must offer highly valuable content and an excellent customer experience. Like most online content, that which can support a fee must be truly premium. It can't be something easily found elsewhere for free.

A paid event is ideal for established events with track records as well as events with extremely valuable content such as access to speakers audiences would rarely hear from or that people need to do their work and that gives them a competitive advantage.

Do you want many more people exposed to your ideas? Make it free!

Hosting a virtual event is an amazing opportunity to expose many more people to your organization's ideas. You might want to consider whether it makes sense to make your virtual event completely free to attendees.

You have the potential to have 10 or 20 times the number of attendees or more. A virtual event that David keynoted in mid-2020 traditionally had about 1,000 attendees when it was in-person. The free virtual event generated over 50,000 registrations and the average attendee watched more than one talk.

Yes, there are expenses associated with hosting a virtual event and if you make it free you will have to cover those costs somehow, perhaps with sponsors, or as part of your marketing budget.

This free approach is ideal for companies that use their event for marketing purposes and to generate sales leads.

A hybrid free and paid approach

Some events offer certain content at no charge while other

content requires a fee to attend. For example, keynotes might be free, while the breakout tracks require a fee. This hybrid (or tiered) model might make most content free but offer premium content or experiences. It could be used to enhance an existing membership or subscription program so that most people can only watch the free content, but these valued customers enjoy premium upgrades.

Another interesting approach is to make the real-time talks at your virtual event free but charge people to replay the content at a later date. This approach also serves to get more people to attend live, which is a great outcome.

A hybrid or tiered approach can be great for industry events where the content is highly valuable, and people are willing to pay for. However, in this model, free content is still available to attract new attendees.

Sponsors

Direct audience revenue is not the only way to support a virtual event. Some have sponsors that pay for an entire event or certain elements of the event.

Simple webinar sponsorship

The sponsored webinar is a very popular type of virtual event. One common model is for a sponsor to pay to have access to present to an established audience. For example, a software vendor might want to reach the members of a membership organization. In this case, the organization works with the sponsor to develop a talk so that will deliver value to the audience to attract and retain them. They also market it to attendees and produce the event. For this access, marketing, and production, the sponsor pays a fee.

Another common approach to this style of webinar is that a company hosts a webinar-style virtual event that features a paid guest speaker. In this case, the company is the sponsor. They host the event, pay for the technology costs, and pay the virtual event speakers' fee. Typically, a speaker on this kind of event is a known personality such as a bestselling author whose book is in related to the sponsor company's business.

Larger events with a single sponsor

Many types of companies and organizations host multi-day, multi-track events with dozens or even hundreds of speakers. Such events can cost hundreds of thousands or millions of dollars to host when you combine all the technology costs, studio costs and speakers' fees.

When one company pays for all of the costs, they are the sole sponsor. This is typically the case when a company hosts a virtual event for its customers.

Larger events or event-series with multiple sponsors

With some larger events, typically those hosted by trade organizations, media companies or associations, there are multiple sponsors. The association organizes the event, often working with companies and sponsors that want to reach the audience of association members, or that the association attracts.

The organizers who put on these events offer companies the ability to pay a fee to be the sponsor of different elements of the event such as an individual speaker, a content track at the event, or a musical guest.

Many sponsors want the ability to speak at the event, or as part of a series of presentations. This makes sense: Your audience is valuable to them and they want the opportunity to deliver a message directly. Organizations that opt to include this in their sponsorship offering must realize that it is critical to work closely with the sponsor to ensure they are not delivering a sales pitch. Rather, it is essential that their participation be held to the same high standards as any other content on the program.

Michelle's tactic here is to help a sponsor see that, by delivering content of value rather than a sales pitch, they demonstrate their expertise in an area important to potential customers. They position themselves as a trusted ally rather than just another company trying to sell them something.

At in-person events, some of the value to the sponsor is usually branding on landing pages, in marketing and promotional materials leading up to the event. That remains true for a virtual event. Being associated with a quality event has value to the brand.

A tried and true sponsor perk at in-person events is for sponsors to be able to provide a branded tchotchke or literature in the swag bag that attendees receive upon registration. Every aspect of the swag bag is typically sponsored with one company paying for the bag itself, another providing the pen, another the notebook and still another the agenda. Each sponsoring company gets their logo stamped on what they paid for as part of the deal.

Some virtual events are experimenting with physical swag bags sent to attendees' homes, so this old school form of sponsorship can still work in the virtual world. Obviously, it will cost more per bag if shipping costs are included compared to handing them out onsite at an in-person event so plan the sponsorship costs and investments accordingly, particularly if you have a far-flung international audience.

However, most sponsors of events want to connect with potential customers. At an in-person event, they can do so at their booth and through networking functions. Here, event organizers need to think digital. You will need to develop ways for sponsors to connect with potential customers and make a lasting impression on attendees.

Like other digital marketing, this might take the form of offering valuable content for those who sign up to request it. It could mean sponsoring a daily recap or highlight reel. It might mean enabling sponsors to meet or connect with attendees in other ways, such as a virtual tradeshow.

We've seen good success with sponsors moderating the Q&A sessions with keynote speakers after the talk with the ability of the sponsor to offer a 30 second overview of their company as part of the deal. If you go this route, make sure the person doing the moderation is skilled at posing good questions and has solid ones prepared in advance, perhaps by working with a member of the event production team.

Marketing and promotion

So, the event is planned, the technology is in place, the speakers are booked, the sponsors are secured, and you are getting close to the big day. Now you need to get as many people registered as possible. It is time to get the word out to as many people as possible and ensure that they have a smooth journey from promo message to post-event survey.

Create a great virtual event page or site

The first step will be to create a web landing page, dedicated webpage, or microsite where all the details of your virtual event are made available. Some event platforms offer integrated pages to host your marketing pages to describe the event. However, you may need to build this yourself and then link to a registration page.

Video on the landing page is a great way to generate interest. One idea is to ask your keynote speakers to film a short (one minute) video that you can use. You might also make a short video highlight reel (two minutes) that is like a movie trailer that you can use to promote the virtual event. Remember, if you are recording sessions in advance, you can use some of the content for this.

You can also ask every speaker a few questions (i.e., "What's one key takeaway you will be sharing in your talk?" "What do you wish you could tell your younger self?" "Who was your biggest professional influence?"), which you record, then edit into a promotional reel or interstitial segments.

Outline the value of your event and how you will offer audiences what they want/need for attending your event. Make this clear and concise. But be sure to illustrate how you are making the most of digital. With your virtual event, attendees are not getting a second-rate experience (where in-person is best). They are getting a first-rate experience that will bring a group of like-minded people together to learn and interact.

Generate links to the landing page in as many ways as you can

Once the landing page is built, link to it from your homepage and any other places on your site, blog, or other web properties.

Ask your employees to put a very short (one sentence) description of the event into their email signatures and include a link to the landing page.

Share links to the landing page on your social networking feeds. Find fans where they live. Engage authentically and invite them to participate.

Social networking from you, your speakers, and partners

As with most marketing, social media provides an excellent channel to promote your virtual event. Depending on the platform, your event hashtag can be an excellent way to rally a community around your topics. You might want to create a calendar of social posts that lead up to the event and build a narrative or reveal exciting new content on a rolling basis. You can share information about each speaker, the topics and more.

You should also tap your partners such as the sponsors of your virtual event (if you have them) and your speakers. Asking speakers to share their participation in your event is an especially valuable way to generate interest. Consider offering them a promo code through which provides their audiences receive a discount or premium experience.

Consider an affiliate program for paid events

If you are running a paid virtual event, you can set up an affiliate program with sponsors and speakers and others so that they generate a commission for every event ticket they sell. Typically, this is done through coupon codes or unique URLs that can be generated in the event platform.

Art and science

If you are new to producing virtual events, the many elements to factor in can seem like a lot to digest. However, what is most interesting to both of us as we have been researching and writing this short book is that there is no hard and fast right way or wrong way to put on a great show. In fact, it is just as much art as it is established science.

We recommend always keeping your audience in mind as you plan your event. What would they want? What's best for them? And here is the ultimate test of your success: Will people become a fan of your event and eagerly sign up for your next one?

CHAPTER 8

The Cost of Producing a Virtual Event

It is possible to host something on a platform like Zoom for a tiny amount of money. It is also possible to spend millions of dollars building a bespoke platform and paying A-list speakers. There are many variables that you need to consider, each with its own costs.

To get you thinking about how the costs add up, we will provide an overview of some of the elements you will need to consider as you make a budget for your virtual event.

Webinar platform costs

The first element of your virtual event to consider is the online platform that you will use to host the event. There are dozens of platform providers to choose from with pricing that ranges from a few hundred dollars to tens of thousands of dollars or more.

Pricing for webinar platforms is typically quoted on a monthly basis per host for an unlimited number of meetings each up to a fixed number of participants.

Here are some pricing options as of mid-2020:

- **Zoom Webinar charges** from $40 per month for one host and up to 100 participants to $6,490 per month for one host and up to 10,000 participants. Discounts are offered if you pay for a year in advance.
- **GoToWebinar charges** from $59 per month for one organizer and 100 participants to $499 per month for one host and up to 3,000 participants. Discounts are offered if you pay for a year in advance. GoToWebinar offers a free seven-day trial.

So, let's say you're planning on running events with one host and up to 1,000 participants each. Zoom charges $140 per month or $1,400 billed annually. Keep in mind that this is a subscription that allows you to produce multiple events throughout the year.

Virtual event platform costs

There are dozens of virtual event platforms (some of which we touch on in Chapter 5). As you look into how they price their services, consider the features that you require. These include things like registration management and reporting, attendee management, social broadcast integration, social promotion, ticketing, credit card processing, chat, polling, breakout rooms, sponsor booths, replays, and so on.

Pricing of these platforms depends on many factors, such as what features you choose and how many participants you will have. Generally speaking, you can expect to pay from $10,000 to

$100,000 and up for each meeting.

However, there are likely other associated costs. For example, if you charge people to attend your virtual event, do not forget to account for credit card processing fees which can be three to five percent of the amount charged, depending on how you handle the processing. Think of the pricing for a platform as à la carte: typically there are many options and you only pay for what you need.

"Think of the platform and costs as like building a website," said TJ Martin, chief executive officer of Cramer, an event and content marketing agency. "There are different elements that come into the equation: What features, size of the audience, and time? Are there exhibitors or sponsors? Do you need breakout rooms? The needs of a program dictate costs. For a large-scale event, the costs of a platform can be $100,000 to $150,000 plus."

Another cost to consider is design of the logo, graphics, and other branding elements for your event.

If you produce recorded video, there will be costs for editing software or an editing service. You may want to add captions or offer transcripts, each adds its own costs.

Also, do not forget to factor in any website design or app development costs, which will also vary depending on your existing resources and what the platform includes.

Virtual event technology and studio costs

If you really want to go first class, you can build out (or rent) a studio to be the home base for your virtual event. That's exactly what Tony Robbins does for all 20 of the multi-day events that he produces in a typical year. David spoke in August 2020 at the first virtual edition of Tony Robbins Business Mastery. He has delivered a talk several times a year at in-person Business Mastery events since 2014. Now that all his events are virtual, Robbins' team created a massive purpose-built studio with a 50-foot around, 20-foot high screen encircling the stage, which displayed several thousand participants on video.

Studio costs vary widely depending on what services you require. A good studio has options to utilize deliver multiple cameras, various sets, the ability to bring in live guests, cutting in recorded video, or coordinating from other studios around the world. To get an idea of what a larger studio looks like, you might watch this short YouTube video discussion between David and TJ Martin from Cramer: *Producing a Virtual Event*.

"We built out state-of-the-art broadcast studio environments for virtual events," said Martin about the company's Boston studio. "They are scalable. We've got a 60-foot by 60-foot studio with multiple cameras, teleprompters, and a full professional staff. If we're doing a live production with the full studio, production costs would be in the neighborhood of $50,000 per day for that type of sophistication. If you don't need to go to that scale, maybe only one speaker with one or two cameras in a small studio environment, that would be significantly less money."

On the lower end, hiring a studio for half a day with one camera and a basic setup to broadcast your content, you might pay $5,000 to $10,000.

Virtual event speaker fees

You will need speakers for your event (a topic David has a strong opinion about, given that he is a professional in-person and virtual keynote speaker). While not every event will have a speaker budget, there are countless benefits to hiring professionals whenever possible and appropriate.

Professional speakers skilled in virtual events can make your event shine. You do not want to invest time and money into gathering an audience, getting the technology in place, and then rely on people who haven't had much experience presenting virtually. Great content in the form of speaker presentations is critical for success.

Virtual speaking fees vary widely. If you are familiar with in-person speaking fees, figure that most virtual speakers are willing to discount their cost for virtual events a bit compared to in-person events because they don't need to travel and therefore the time commitment is shorter. However, there is still considerable prep time, rehearsals, promotion and so on that you are paying for as part of the fee.

Note that you will not have the expense of transporting the

speaker to your event (flights, car service, hotel, etc.) and they are generally more flexible on fees given that they do not have to travel.

A virtual event speaker who has several years of experience and positive endorsements from event planners they have worked in the past might start at a few thousand dollars for an appearance.

For a well-known speaker such as a celebrity, professional athlete, or *Wall Street Journal* or *New York Times* bestselling author, fees likely start at around $10,000 and can go up quickly, well past $100,000, depending on how well-known the person is. To research professional speakers, you may want to work with a member of the International Association of Speakers Bureaus.

Yes, you can find people who will speak for free. Often, a no-cost speaker will want to sell something to your audience. Or they are beginners just trying to get some experience.

However, there are also subject matter experts or industry figures you will want to include on your program who have limited speaking experience, particularly for virtual events. You will need to factor in the time and effort it takes to help these speakers deliver their best talk. One way to address this might be to hire expert interviewers for a virtual fireside chat format.

CHAPTER 9

How to Run A Great Virtual Event

There is a lot to consider when running a virtual event. We hope we have provided you with some valuable background information as you think about putting together your own virtual event. As with any business initiative, there are a wide range of factors and considerable planning that will help contribute to your success.

Identify your goals and measure success

Very early in your virtual event planning, you should consider what the goals are for putting the event on. Is this a revenue stream? Is it primarily to build fans of your organization? Or are you using it to generate leads to sell a product or service?

Revenue generator

For some organizations, a paid event makes the most sense. A paid event is ideal for established events with track records as well as events with highly valuable content that people need to do their work. One key challenge will be figuring out what the right price to charge will be. Consider what similar events charge, the relative value of and scarcity of your content, and the revenue you need to earn to cover costs and generate a profit.

Another way to bring in virtual event revenue, often used by those hosted by trade organizations or associations, is to sell sponsorships. These organizations may offer the content as a member or subscriber benefit, but then cover costs with sponsorship sales. While profits are not likely to be the key objective, keeping an eye on cost is always a factor. That said, sponsors expect attendees (usually in the form of sales leads). It is essential that you create sufficient value and a marketing plan that will attract attendees to your event.

Building fans of your organization

Hosting a virtual event is an amazing opportunity to have many more people exposed to your organizations ideas than was possible with in-person events. As such, you might want to consider if it makes sense to make your virtual event completely free to attendees.

If your event is free, you may be surprised at the number of people who register. It's important to set a goal and monitor the number of registrations because some platforms charge based on how many people participate.

A problem with free events is that many people sign up but then don't show for the event. You will need to send emails to remind people they signed up for a free event and tell them what to expect, reinforcing the benefits of attending. It is also a good idea for registration confirmation to include a reminder that automatically adds the event to their calendar.

Generating sales leads

Some organizations use virtual events to expose new people to their products and services with the hope of generating sales leads. This approach is often used by companies in industries like technology, travel, health and wellness, real estate, and financial services. The event is free to participate and usually there is a guest speaker who is a draw for people to register.

However, registrations are not everything. Though they can generate good leads, registrants that do not attend are less likely to be highly engaged. Ensure that you create incentives to turn up the day of the event. You may also want to put archived event content behind a registration wall to collect information that will help you turn registrants into customers.

We recommend that you have three goals if you are using your virtual event to generate sales leads. These include setting: 1) A goal for how many people you expect to register for the event, 2) A goal for how many people will express interest in learning more after the event, and 3) The expected number of sales at some point in the future based on running the event.

Big picture planning

There are a lot of moving parts to putting on a virtual event. We have included many, but not all, in these pages. Here are some ways to keep the big picture in focus.

Create a checklist

Many event planners say that there are two keys to managing all of it: Creating a checklist of things that need to get done and a timeline for when you need to do them.

The checklist will include such things as:

- Developing your objectives and Key Performance Indicators
- Choosing the platform to host the event
- Establishing pricing
- Building the event website (and app, if applicable)
- Social media planning including the #hashtag
- Picking the date(s)
- Hiring keynote speakers
- Finding panel moderators
- Selecting panelists
- Securing sponsors
- Creating a marketing plan, including social media promotion
- Creating speaker prep materials and guidelines
- Scheduling and hosting speaker prep sessions
- Building networking and interactive elements
- And much more!

Your event timeline

You will also want to create an event timeline that uses "day zero" as the start of the event and works backwards from there to include all of the things you need to do from your checklist identified by when it will be done.

For example, you might set a deadline for six months out from day zero to select the date, five months out to select the platform and four months out to select keynote speakers.

You will also want to work forward from day zero to plan things such as handling the event replays (if you have them), thanking people who participated, and getting the next year's event onto the calendar.

And then the whole cycle will start again.

It's go time

Whenever there is a major disruption in a marketplace, opportunity presents itself to those who are willing to embrace change. When news and information moved from offline to online in the past decades, it meant those who jumped in quickly were able to get a head start. Huge companies like Google, Facebook, and Twitter were established but so were thousands of smaller businesses.

Less obvious were the organizations that made the switch to digital marketing early, creating content rich websites, blogs, video channels, and social media feeds before their competitors. Those who experimented and innovated took an early lead. They frequently grew more quickly as they were ahead of the curve on experiences and were viewed as leaders.

We are in an unparalleled time in the events business. In-person events are few and far between as we write this. But the opportunity for those who leap into the world of virtual events is huge.

Right now, you have what may be a once in a career opportunity to grow and prosper with virtual events while others are waiting for the world to return to "normal."

We don't think there will be a total return to what once was. Yes, in-person events will return, no question about it. But as virtual events deliver great experiences for participants and benefits to the organizations that host them, their role will be cemented. In fact, we believe the future holds promise for a hybrid approach to events where some people experience the content in-person while others have a virtual experience.

This is an opportunity. Do not miss your chance to create experiences your audience will truly love.

Now is the time. Now is your time.

Acknowledgements

We would like to thank Doug Eymer for designing the wonderful cover. We didn't know what we wanted but we knew it needed to capture the spirit of *Standout Virtual Events*. Doug nailed it.

Copy editor Michelle Anya Anjirbag read every word of the manuscript and provided suggestions to make it better, for which we are both highly appreciative. — *David & Michelle*

To my long-time industry pal, Michelle Manafy: Thank you for agreeing to write this book with me. It's great to "get the band back together" and work together once again.

A particularly heartfelt thank you to Tony D'Amelio who manages my relationships with speakers bureaus and provides invaluable advice on how to make my talks better.

My literary agent, Margret McBride, and her colleague Faye Atchison are instrumental in helping me navigate the arcane world of publishing books. Thank you, Margret and Faye!

Nick Morgan and Michael Port have advised me on my speaking techniques. Their help has been essential as I've developed my speaking style over more than a decade – thank you both.

I am grateful to Tony Robbins for bringing me into the Business Mastery community, where I present several times a year, delivering my New Marketing Mastery program. I have learned a great deal about how to build fans from Tony.

Thank you to Michelle Gustafsson who works with me on my customer service and provides valuable advice on many aspects of my speaking work.

David Jackel and Shana Bethune worked with me on some of the wonderful videos we refer to in this book.

The team at IMPACT, especially Bob Ruffolo and Brian Casey, make me look way better than I deserve by providing amazing advice on my online marketing.

David Levitsky helped me with some early drafts of the ideas that made it into these pages.

I am super grateful to the many people who have booked me to speak over the years including event planners and speakers bureau representatives. If you want to hire a great speaker, please reach out to a bureau that is a member of the International Association of Speakers Bureaus.

To Yukari Watanabe Scott, my wife of thirty years and our daughter Allison Carolyn Reiko Goulet-Scott, M.D. thank you for enthusiastically supporting all of my projects. — *David*

To one of the coolest guys in the business, David Meerman Scott: I forgot how fun work can be. Thank you for thinking of me for this book and for the energy and creativity you bring to every project.

I can not thank the DCN team enough for the collaboration and deep expertise you share with me every day — on our events, and all the work we do to support the stellar companies our organization represents. And I must acknowledge those same companies for working with me to create the content for our member events and for their willingness to share candid insights about their own events' businesses.

I appreciate the many event organizers who worked with me on in-person and virtual event sessions over the years. I have learned so much from every experience and appreciate all of them.

And, of course, I could not be more grateful to have the support of my family — Harlequin and Daniel Sullivan — in this and every endeavor. — *Michelle*

About The Authors

David Meerman Scott is a marketing and business growth strategist, entrepreneur, advisor to emerging companies, author and public speaker.

He spotted the real-time marketing revolution in its infancy and wrote five books about it including *The New Rules of Marketing and PR*, now in a seventh edition, with more than 400,000 copies sold in English and available in 29 languages from Albanian to Vietnamese. His most recent *Wall Street Journal* bestselling book, *Fanocracy: Turning Fans into Customers and Customers into Fans*, written with his daughter Reiko, was released in early 2020 from Portfolio / Penguin Random House.

David considers speaking his art. He cannot sing, dance, or play a musical instrument, but he loves to perform on a stage or at a virtual event. He's delivered in-person events in 46 countries and on all seven continents and has delivered presentations at hundreds of virtual events.

Standout Virtual Events is his 12th book.

Learn more about David or contact him at
www.davidmeermanscott.com

Follow him on Twitter @DMScott

Michelle Manafy learned to use a computer (DOS based) in journalism school at San Francisco State University. A few months later, she became the computer lab monitor as part of her work study. Despite learning her keyboard skills on a manual typewriter, Michelle whole-heartedly embraced the digital transformation of her craft. Now, she is an expert on the business and technology of digital media.

Currently, Michelle serves as the editorial director of Digital Content Next (DCN), the only trade organization dedicated to serving the unique and diverse needs of high-quality digital media companies. In this role, Michelle is responsible for DCN's content-related initiatives, including its InContext site, social media presence as well as the organization's technology, product development, and video events.

As a speaker and writer, she promotes industry best-practices in a wide range of venues. Michelle is a regular contributor to *Inc.com* and her career has included leadership roles at the *Media Industry Newsletter* (min), UK-based digital publisher FreePint Limited, and Information Today, Inc.

Learn more about Michelle or contact her at digitalcontentnext.org/blog/dcn-staff/michelle-manafy/

Follow her on Twitter @michellemanafy

Printed in Great Britain
by Amazon